LIGHTHOUSES
of New England™

Designs by Connie Rand

HOUSE of
WHITE
BIRCHES

PUBLISHERS
SINCE 1947

Lights Along the Shore

Wherever ocean waves meet the shore, you'll find lighthouses built to protect ships at sea from coming too close to land. New England's long and complicated coastline requires many of these imposing beacons.

The view from Owl's Head Light.

Beach roses grow near Dice Head Light in Castine, Maine. This light is now a private residence.

Within a day's drive of my home in Maine, there are more than 60 lighthouses. Some are on tiny islands. Others can be found at the end of a narrow road that twists to the shore. Some are now private residences with their service to marine traffic a distant memory, but most are still operational. The oldest one depicted on the quilt in this book is Portland Head Light, commissioned in 1791 by George Washington and still standing watch over Casco Bay.

The Owl's Head Light has a steep staircase leading to the tower.

I've been a quilter since 1991. That was my first year working for House of White Birches as a technical illustrator for their quilting publications. I soon began designing my own quilts, an extension of my training as a painter. During my art-school days, Portland Head Light was a favorite sketching location.

In preparation for this book, my husband Lee and I traveled to most of the lighthouses you see on the quilt. His photos show the beauty and variety of the lighthouses of the New England coast.

West Quoddy Head Light in Lubec, Maine, is located on a point of land that is the first place in the United States to see the morning sun. The lighthouse is often shrouded in fog.

A boat crosses the harbor in this distant view of Owl's Head Light from the breakwater in Rockland, Maine.

Meet the Designer
Connie Rand

Connie Rand has been a technical artist for House of White Birches quilting publications since 1991. She has a degree in Fine Arts from the Maine College of Art in Portland, Maine.

She specializes in wildlife art, and her work can be found in collections across the country and in Canada. Fabric has joined pencil, ink and paint as a form of artistic expression for Connie.

Connie and her husband Lee live in Lincoln, Maine, where they own an advertising agency, and have a Web site about their hometown: www.lincolnmaine.us.

General Instructions For Appliqué

Full-size patterns are included for each appliquéd lighthouse design. Use your favorite method of hand or machine appliqué to complete the designs. Basic information and hints to help you successfully complete the blocks are given here. Read through these instructions before starting your blocks and refer to them as necessary.

PREPARING FOR APPLIQUÉ

Fold the background squares and rectangles in quarters and press to crease centerlines as shown in Figure 1. Lightly trace the pattern on the background piece using a water-erasable marker or chalk pencil, aligning the creased lines on the background piece with the center of the pattern as shown in Figure 2. Trace only enough lines to help place the appliqué shapes as shown in Figure 3; do not trace every detail of the pattern. **Note:** *For triangle blocks, align the pattern edges with the edges of the background triangle.*

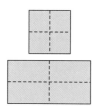

Figure 1

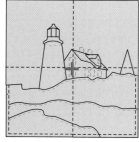

Figure 2

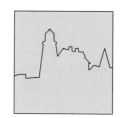

Figure 3

A number identifies each shape within a block as shown in Figure 4.

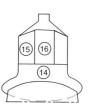 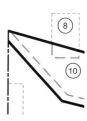

Figure 4   **Figure 5**

When preparing templates and fabric pieces for either hand or machine appliqué, be sure to include the section of a piece that will be overlapped by an adjacent piece. This section is outlined with long gray dashed lines on the pattern as shown in Figure 5.

Different line styles on the drawings identify overlapped pieces, placement of pieces or pattern sections and the outside edge of each piece. Figure 6 shows each line included in these patterns and an example of its use.

Hand Appliqué

For traditional hand appliqué, prepare a finished-size template from plastic for each shape. For pieces on the outside edges of blocks that have the seam allowance already marked, include the marked seam allowance in the template. Trace the plastic templates on the chosen fabric's right side, allowing about ½" between pieces as shown in Figure 7. Cut out the pieces, adding a ⅛"–¼" seam allowance to all edges, except those that already include the seam allowance. Turn under and hand-baste the seam allowance of each piece, except those that will be overlapped by

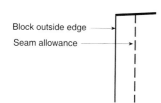

Block outside edge
Seam allowance

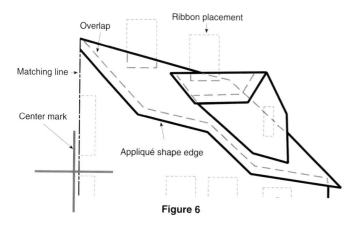

Overlap

Ribbon placement

Matching line

Center mark

Appliqué shape edge

Figure 6

½"

Figure 7

another piece and those on the outside edges of the block, or leave seam allowances to needle-turn as you appliqué the pieces.

For freezer-paper appliqué, photocopy or trace the design on a sheet of paper. Place the design side against a light box or bright window and trace the pieces on the paper side of freezer paper. Press the freezer-paper templates on the wrong side of the chosen fabric with a hot dry iron, leaving space between pieces as shown in Figure 8. Cut out the pieces, adding a ⅛"–¼" seam allowance to all edges, except those that already include the seam allowance. Press the seam allowance under using the edge of the freezer paper as a guide, except on those pieces that will be overlapped by another piece and those on the outside edges of the block. Hand-baste in place through all layers to hold.

Note: *The Lighthouses of New England quilt used the freezer-paper appliqué method.*

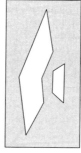

Figure 8

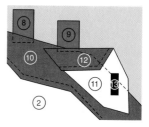

Figure 9

The piece numbers determine the order in which the pieces will be appliquéd to the background. Beginning with the lowest number, pin the pieces in place on the background in numerical order, overlapping pieces as indicated on the pattern as shown in Figure 9.

Blind-stitch the pieces in place, using thread to match the appliqué piece and turning under seam allowances, if necessary. Remove seam-allowance basting.

For freezer-paper pieces, cut a small slit in the background fabric behind each appliquéd piece as shown in Figure 10. Remove the freezer-paper piece using small tweezers. Or, remove the paper after pressing and before stitching. This is best for small pieces since there is not enough space to cut the slit and remove paper from the back side.

Figure 10

Figure 11

If darker pieces show through lighter top pieces, cut a slit through the background behind the darker piece and trim away the section of the darker piece that is overlapped by the lighter piece, leaving only a narrow seam allowance as shown in Figure 11. Trim the darker portion of the seam allowance, if necessary.

Press the appliquéd design.

Machine Appliqué

Bond lightweight fusible interfacing to the wrong side of any light-color fabrics to prevent shadowing of darker fabrics.

Prepare a template from plastic for each piece in the design. Flip each template and trace the pieces to be cut from each fabric in a group on the paper side of fusible web, leaving space between each fabric group and marking the number of each piece on the traced outline as shown in Figure 12. Instead of making templates, you may photocopy or trace the pattern onto another sheet of paper. Place the design side against a light box or bright window and trace the pieces to be cut directly onto the fusible web, again grouping each fabric's pieces and marking the number on the traced outline.

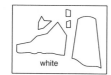

white

Figure 12

Roughly cut out each group of pieces, leaving a margin around each group. Fuse each group to the wrong side of the chosen fabrics following the manufacturer's instructions. Cut out each piece on the drawn line.

Beginning with the lowest-numbered piece, remove the paper backing and arrange the pieces on the background in numerical order, overlapping pieces as indicated on the pattern. When satisfied with the arrangement, fuse pieces to the background fabric.

You may find it easier to fuse small sections of a pattern that has many pieces. Arrange one section in numerical order and fuse the pieces as shown in Figure 13. Move on to the next section and do the same. Continue fusing sections until the design is complete. Just remember to not only fuse the pieces within a section in numerical order, but to also fuse the pieces for the whole design in numerical order. Otherwise, you may find that you have fused a piece in one section that should have overlapped or been overlapped by a piece in another section.

Figure 13

Cut a piece of fabric stabilizer large enough to fit behind the fused design. Fuse or pin it in place on the wrong side of the background piece.

Use all-purpose thread, machine-embroidery thread or rayon thread to match each appliqué piece in the top of your machine and all-purpose thread to match the background in the bobbin. Satin-stitch around the edges of each piece using a close medium-width stitch. Adjust your machine as necessary to prevent the bobbin thread from pulling to the top of your block.

Use a press cloth to press the appliquéd design.

Ribbon Details

Use ribbon to add small details such as windows, railings, chimneys and fence posts. Placement of ribbon pieces is marked on the patterns with blue dashed lines.

Cut a piece of ribbon in the width and length of the pattern pieces. Apply seam sealant to each end to prevent fraying.

Hand-stitch the ribbon in place on the block using thread to match the ribbon. ■

Lighthouses of New England

For as long as people have been going to sea, they have made beacons on the shore to mark dangerous places. The powerful lights keep ships off the rocky New England coast as they have been doing for centuries. This quilt brings these symbols of safety into your home.

PROJECT SPECIFICATIONS

Skill Level: Advanced
Quilt Size: 64" x 92"
Block Size: 12" x 12", 12" x 22", 23" x 23" and
  24" x 24" x 34"
Number of Blocks: 11

FABRIC & BATTING

- Large scraps green, rust, red, dark red, black, light rust and light, medium and dark gray for lighthouse appliqué
- ¼ yard each 3 rock prints
- ¼ yard water print
- ¼ yard dark brown mottled
- ¼ yard tan/brown mottled
- ¼ yard tan/green print
- ¼ yard bright green tonal
- ¼ yard green/black mottled
- ⅜ yard green speckle print
- ½ yard green mottled
- ¾ yard white tonal
- 2¼ yards total blue-sky prints
- 2¾ yards red mottled
- 3⅛ yards dark blue mottled
- Backing 70" x 98"
- Batting 70" x 98"

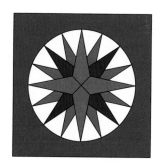

Mariner's Compass
23" x 23" Block

SUPPLIES & TOOLS

- All-purpose thread to match fabrics
- Quilting thread
- ½ yard ⅜"-wide white grosgrain ribbon
- ½ yard each ⅛"-wide black and white satin ribbon
- 1 yard each ⅜"- and ½"-wide red and black grosgrain ribbon
- Seam sealant
- Freezer paper
- Water-erasable marker or chalk pencil
- String
- Basic sewing tools and supplies

INSTRUCTIONS
Cutting

1. Cut one 23½" x 23½" E square dark blue mottled.

2. Cut two 5½" x 64½" Q strips and two 5½" x 82½" P strips along the remaining length of the dark blue mottled.

3. Cut four 12⅞" x 12⅞" I squares from the remaining width of the dark blue mottled. Cut each I square in half on one diagonal to make eight I triangles.

4. Cut four 12½" x 12½" J squares and two 12½" x 22½" K rectangles blue-sky prints.

5. Cut two 24⅞" x 24⅞" squares blue-sky prints; cut each square in half on one diagonal to make four L triangles.

6. Cut two 2½" x 50½" M strips, two 2½" x 54½" O strips and two 2½" x 78½" N strips along the length of the red mottled.

7. Cut two 2" x 23½" F strips, two 2" x 26½" G strips and eight 2½" x 12½" H strips from the remaining width of the red mottled.

8. Prepare templates for the Mariner's Compass block using A–D patterns given; cut as directed on each piece.

9. Cut eight 2¼" by fabric width strips red mottled for binding.

Completing the Mariner's Compass Block

1. To piece one Mariner's Compass block, sew D to opposite sides of C as shown in Figure 1; repeat for eight C-D units. Press seams in one direction.

Figure 1

2. Sew a C-D unit to opposite sides of B as shown in Figure 2; repeat for four B-C-D units. Press seams in one direction.

Figure 2

3. Join the four A pieces, stopping stitching at the end of the marked seam allowance as shown in Figure 3. Set in the B-C-D units between the A points to complete the A unit as shown in Figure 4; press seams in one direction.

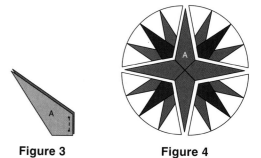

Figure 3   **Figure 4**

4. Fold the E square in half and crease to mark the vertical and horizontal centers.

5. Tie the string around the chalk pencil; cut string to make a 9" length.

6. Place the end of the string in the center of E and secure with finger. Extend string and pencil and draw a circle on the E square. The circle should measure 18" in diameter.

7. Trim the circle away from the E square ¼" from marked line as shown in Figure 5. Turn the edge of circle under along marked line; baste to hold.

Figure 5

8. Center E over the pieced A unit, aligning A points with crease marks on E; hand-appliqué in place to complete the Mariner's Compass block.

Completing the Center Unit

1. Sew F strips to opposite sides of the Mariner's Compass block and G strips to the remaining sides; press seams toward F and G strips.

2. Sew an H strip between two I triangles as shown in Figure 6; press seams toward H. Repeat for four H-I units.

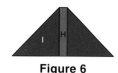

Figure 6

3. Sew an H-I unit to each side of the bordered center as shown in Figure 7; press seams toward H-I units.

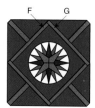

Figure 7

Appliqué Blocks

1. Prepare a complete pattern for each lighthouse block referring to the pattern diagrams for joining sections.

2. Refer to the General Instructions for Appliqué on page 4 to make the Prospect Harbor Light, Pemaquid Point Light, Fort Point Light and Dice Head Light blocks using J background squares. Repeat with K rectangles to make the Pumpkin Island Light and Portland Head Light blocks.

3. Complete the triangle lighthouse blocks using L triangles, again referring to the General Instructions for Appliqué on page 4.

Completing the Top

1. Sew a triangle lighthouse block to each side of the quilt center as shown in Figure 8; press seams toward blocks.

Figure 8

2. Join one K and two J lighthouse blocks with two H strips to make the top and bottom rows referring to Figure 9; press seams toward H strips.

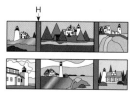

Figure 9

3. Join the top and bottom rows with the quilt center and M strips to complete the pieced center referring to the Placement Diagram for positioning; press seams toward M strips.

4. Sew N strips to opposite long sides and O strips to the top and bottom of the pieced center; press seams toward N and O strips.

5. Sew P strips to opposite sides and Q strips to the top and bottom of the pieced center to complete the top; press seams toward P and Q strips.

Completing the Quilt

1. Sandwich batting between the completed top and prepared backing piece; pin or baste layers together to hold flat.

2. Quilt as desired by hand or machine.

3. When quilting is complete, remove pins or

basting; trim batting and backing edges even with quilt top.

4. Join binding strips on short ends to make one long strip; press seams open.

5. Fold binding strip in half with wrong sides together along length; press.

6. Sew binding strip to quilt top with raw edges even, mitering corners and overlapping ends. Turn binding to the back side; hand- or machine-stitch in place to finish. ■

Lighthouses of New England
Placement Diagram
64" x 92"

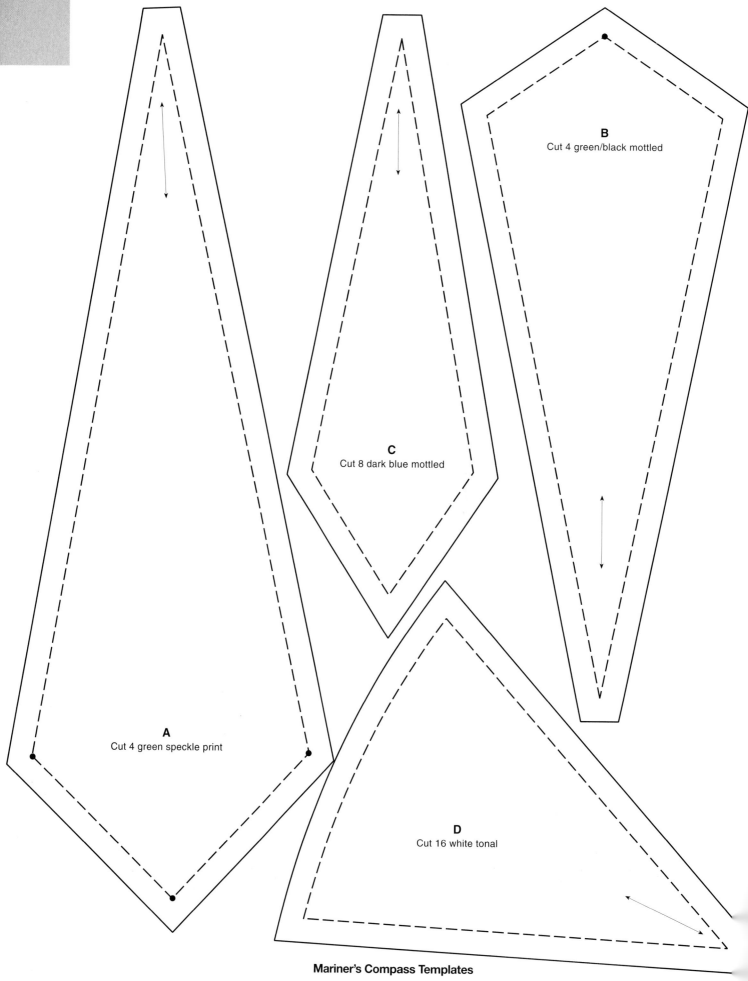

B
Cut 4 green/black mottled

C
Cut 8 dark blue mottled

A
Cut 4 green speckle print

D
Cut 16 white tonal

Mariner's Compass Templates

Prospect Harbor Point Light

Pospect Harbor Point Light
Prospect Harbor, Maine

Constructed in 1891

Automated in 1951

Operational (U.S. Coast Guard)

38 feet high

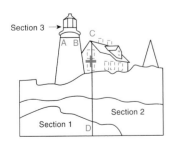

Prospect Harbor Point Light
Pattern Diagram

Line Key

Appliqué shape edge ━━━━

Block outside edge ───

Seam allowance ─ ─ ─ ─

Overlap ─ ── ─ ── ─

Matching line ──·──·──·──

Ribbon placement ·············

Center mark ┼

Prospect Harbor Point Light
12" x 12" Block

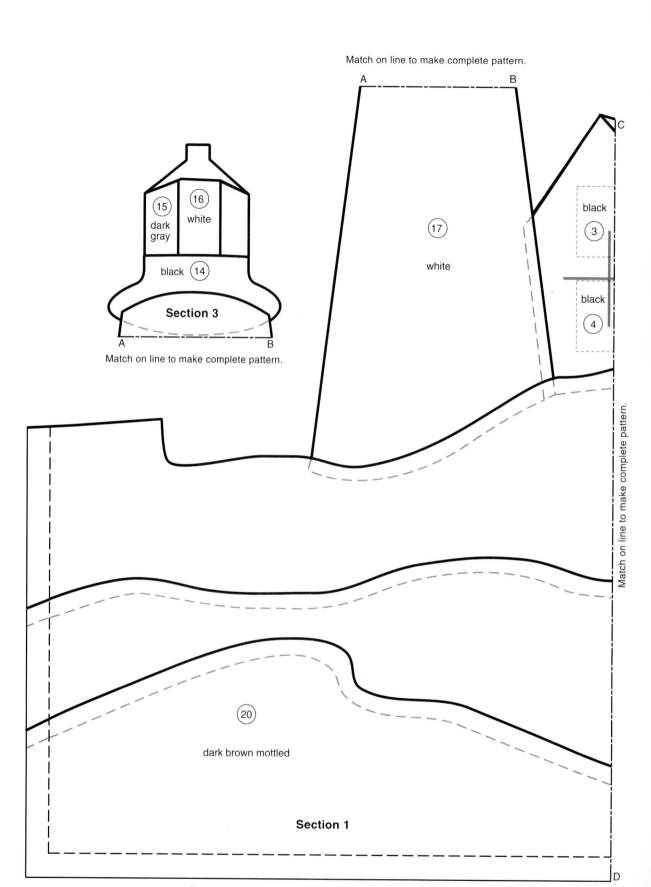

Match on line to make complete pattern.

A   B

C

black
③

black
④

15
dark gray

16
white

black ⑭

Section 3

A   B

Match on line to make complete pattern.

⑰
white

Match on line to make complete pattern.

⑳
dark brown mottled

Section 1

D

Prospect Harbor Point Light Appliqué Pattern

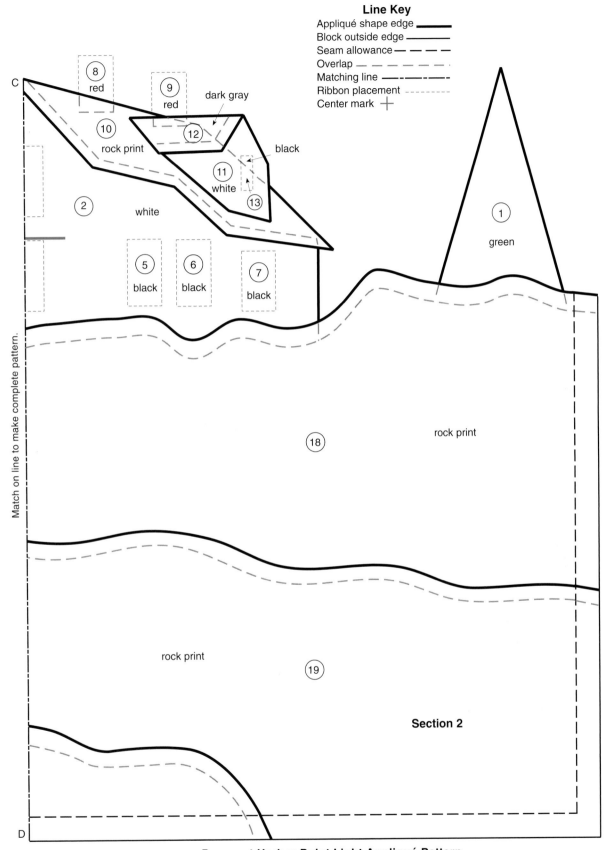

Line Key
Appliqué shape edge ——————
Block outside edge ——————
Seam allowance — — — —
Overlap — — — —
Matching line —··—··—
Ribbon placement ············
Center mark +

Section 2

Prospect Harbor Point Light Appliqué Pattern

Match on line to make complete pattern.

Pumpkin Island Light

**Pumpkin Island Light
Sargentville, Maine**

Constructed in 1854

Deactivated in 1933 (private owner)

28 feet high

Line Key

Appliqué shape edge ━━━━
Block outside edge ─────
Seam allowance — — — —
Overlap – — — — — ·
Matching line ——·——·——
Ribbon placement ----------
Center mark +

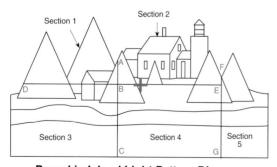

Pumpkin Island Light Pattern Diagram

Pumpkin Island Light
12" x 22" Block

HOUSE OF WHITE BIRCHES, BERNE, INDIANA 46711 WWW.WHITEBIRCHES.COM

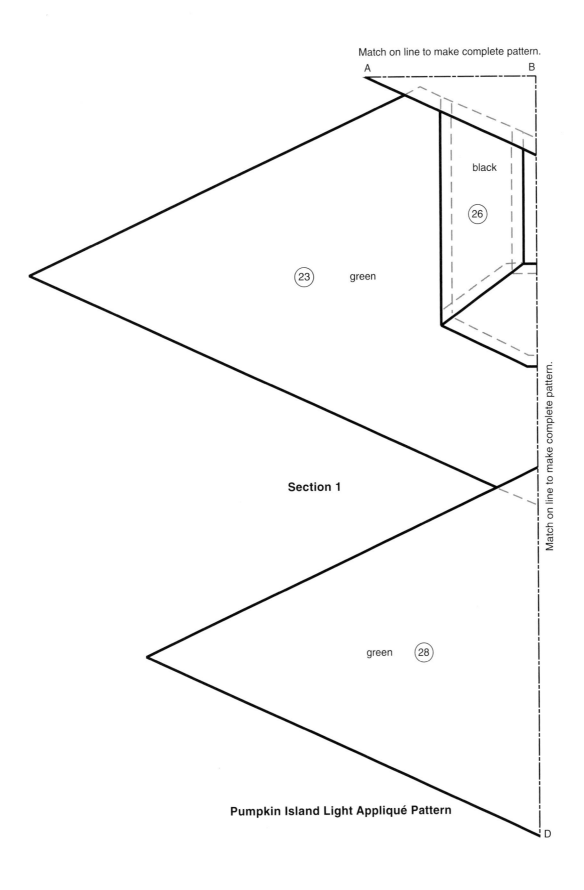

Match on line to make complete pattern.

A   B

black

(26)

(23)   green

Match on line to make complete pattern.

Section 1

green   (28)

Pumpkin Island Light Appliqué Pattern

D

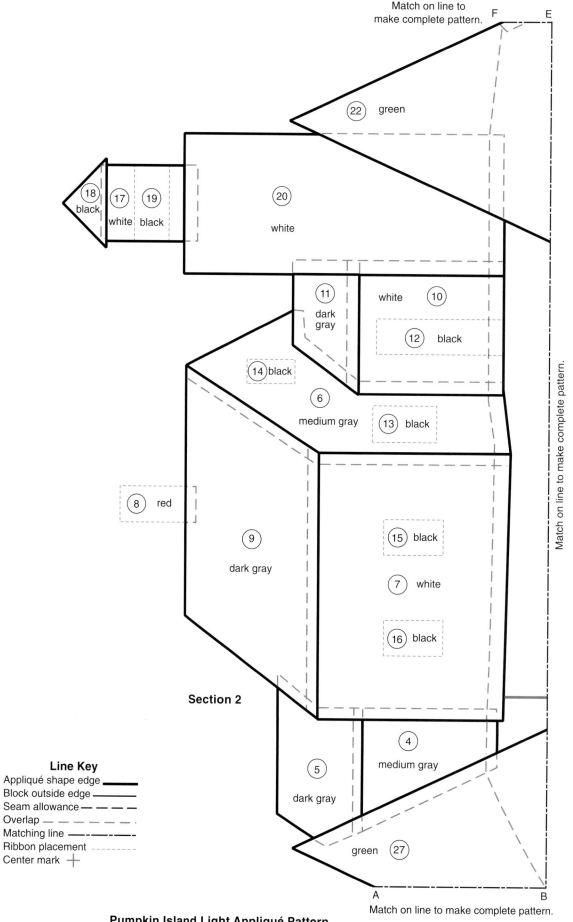

Match on line to make complete pattern.

(22) green

(18) black
(17) white
(19) black
(20) white

(11) dark gray
white (10)
(12) black

(14) black
(6)
medium gray
(13) black

(8) red

(9) dark gray

(15) black
(7) white
(16) black

Section 2

Match on line to make complete pattern.

(4) medium gray

(5) dark gray

green (27)

Line Key
Appliqué shape edge ━━━━
Block outside edge ────
Seam allowance ─ ─ ─ ─
Overlap ─ ─ ─ ─ ─
Matching line ─ ∙ ─ ∙ ─ ∙
Ribbon placement ∙∙∙∙∙∙∙∙
Center mark ✛

Match on line to make complete pattern.

Pumpkin Island Light Appliqué Pattern

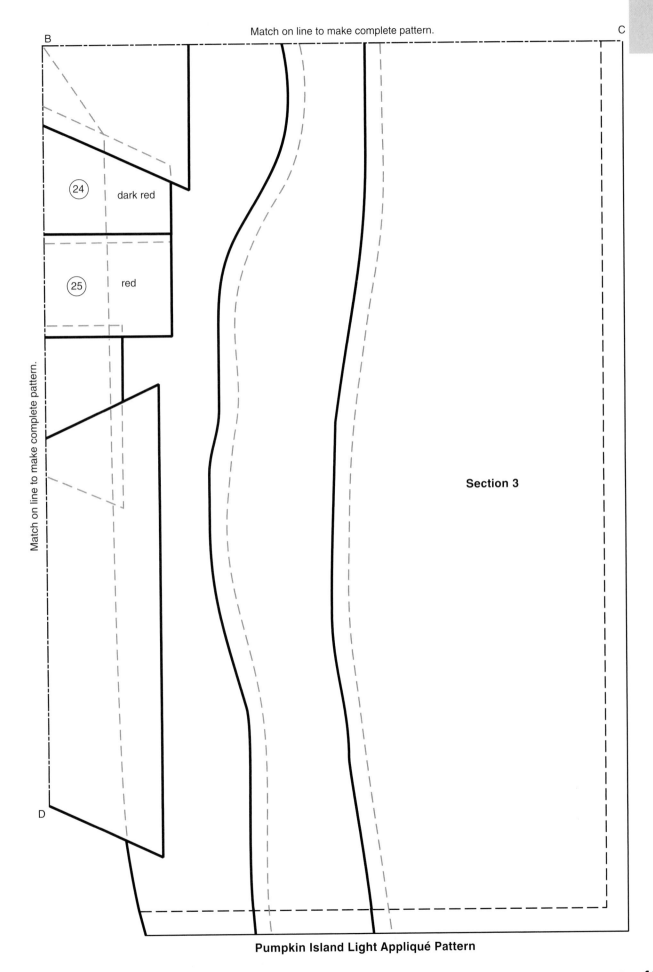

Match on line to make complete pattern.

B

C

Match on line to make complete pattern.

24 dark red

25 red

Section 3

D

Pumpkin Island Light Appliqué Pattern

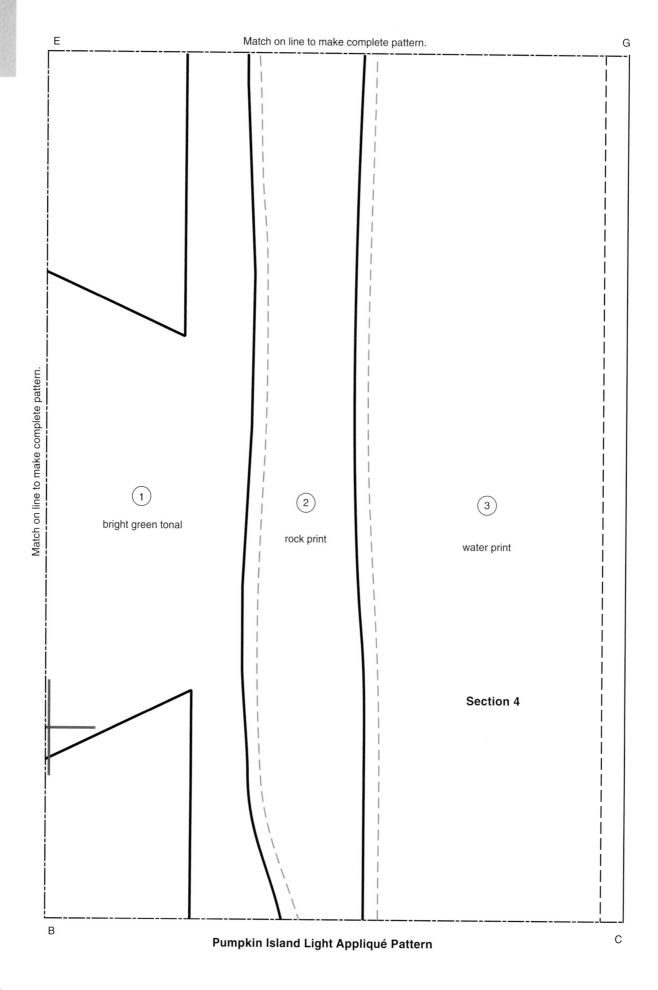

E   Match on line to make complete pattern.   G

Match on line to make complete pattern.

1
bright green tonal

2
rock print

3
water print

Section 4

B

Pumpkin Island Light Appliqué Pattern

C

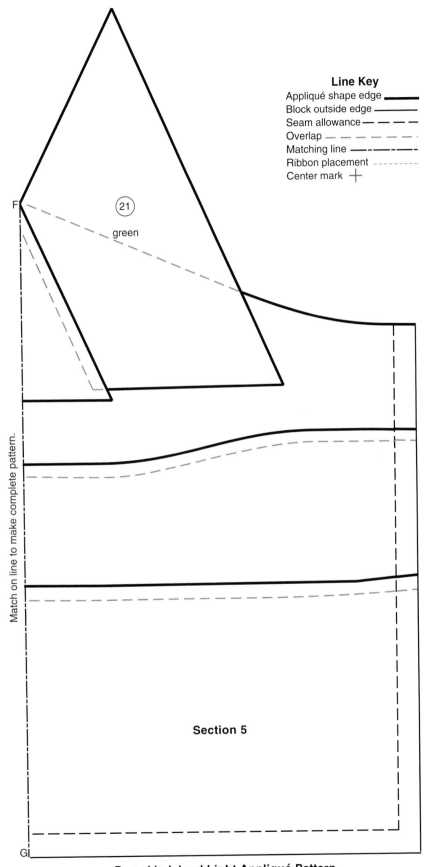

Line Key

Appliqué shape edge ——————
Block outside edge ————
Seam allowance — — — —
Overlap — — — —
Matching line —·—·—·—
Ribbon placement ---------
Center mark +

F

㉑

green

Match on line to make complete pattern.

Section 5

G

Pumpkin Island Light Appliqué Pattern

West Quoddy Head Light

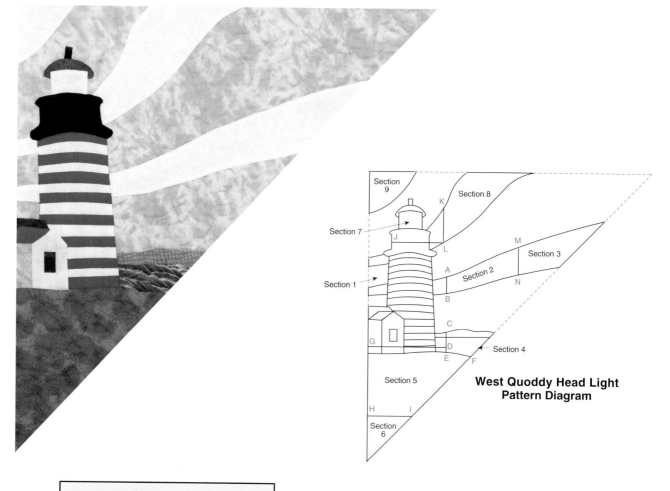

**West Quoddy Head Light
Pattern Diagram**

**West Quoddy Head Light
Lubec, Maine**
Constructed in 1808
Operational (West Quoddy Head State Park)
49 feet high
Lubec is the first place in the United States to
see the sunrise. This lighthouse has striking
red and white stripes going around the tower.
The number of stripes has varied over the years
from one repainting to the next.

Line Key
Appliqué shape edge ▬▬▬▬
Block outside edge ————
Seam allowance — — — —
Overlap — — — — —
Matching line —·—·—·—
Ribbon placement --------

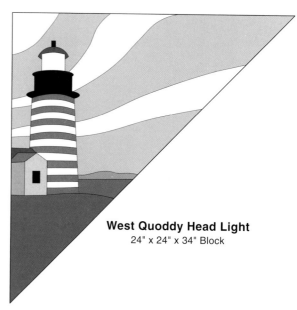

West Quoddy Head Light
24" x 24" x 34" Block

HOUSE OF WHITE BIRCHES, BERNE, INDIANA 46711   WWW.WHITEBIRCHES.COM

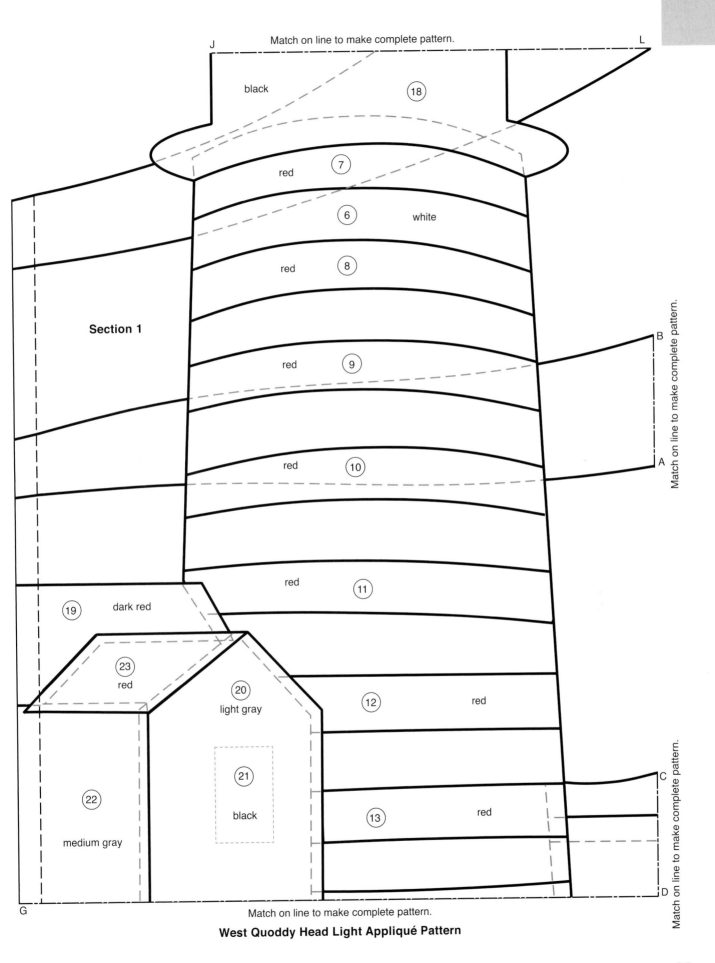

Match on line to make complete pattern.

J · L

black

⑱

red ⑦

⑥ white

red ⑧

Section 1

red ⑨

B

Match on line to make complete pattern.

red ⑩

A

red ⑪

⑲ dark red

⑳ light gray

red ⑫

red

⑫ red

㉓ red

㉒

㉑ black

⑬ red

C

Match on line to make complete pattern.

medium gray

D

G

Match on line to make complete pattern.

West Quoddy Head Light Appliqué Pattern

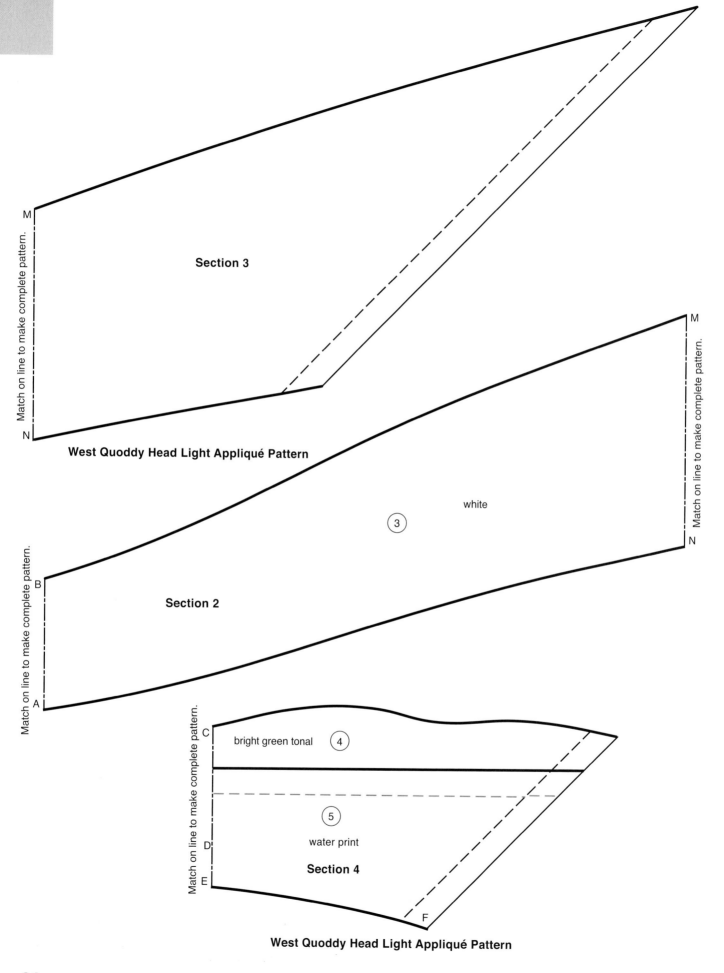

Section 3

Match on line to make complete pattern.

M

N

West Quoddy Head Light Appliqué Pattern

M

Match on line to make complete pattern.

N

white

③

B

Section 2

Match on line to make complete pattern.

A

Match on line to make complete pattern.

C

bright green tonal ④

D

⑤

water print

E

Section 4

F

West Quoddy Head Light Appliqué Pattern

HOUSE OF WHITE BIRCHES, BERNE, INDIANA 46711   WWW.WHITEBIRCHES.COM

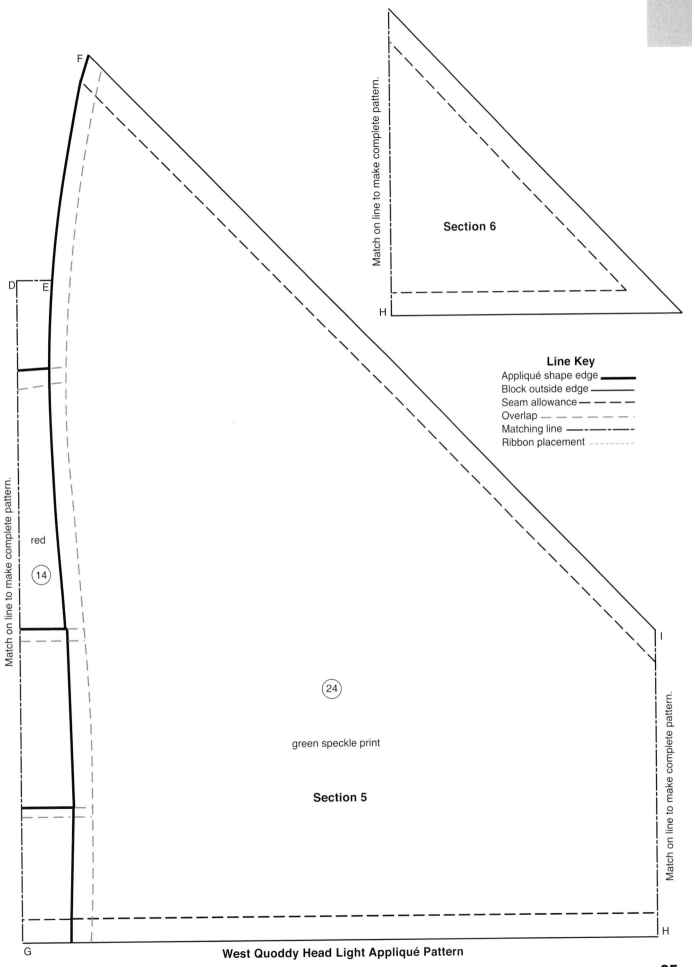

Match on line to make complete pattern.

Section 6

Line Key
Appliqué shape edge ————
Block outside edge ————
Seam allowance — — — —
Overlap — — — —
Matching line —·—·—·—
Ribbon placement ·········

D   E

Match on line to make complete pattern.

red

(14)

F

(24)

green speckle print

Section 5

I

Match on line to make complete pattern.

H

G   H

West Quoddy Head Light Appliqué Pattern

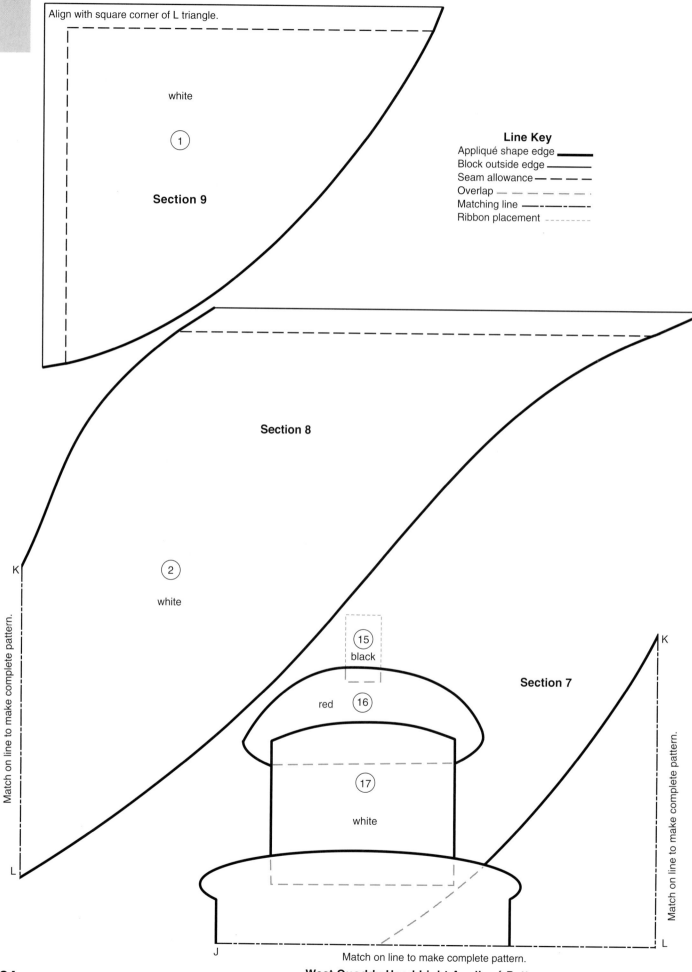

Align with square corner of L triangle.

white

(1)

Section 9

Line Key
Appliqué shape edge ▬▬▬▬
Block outside edge ────────
Seam allowance ── ── ──
Overlap ─ ─ ─ ─ ─
Matching line ─ ∙ ─ ∙ ─
Ribbon placement ∙∙∙∙∙∙∙∙

Section 8

K

(2)

white

(15)
black

red   (16)

Section 7

K

(17)

white

Match on line to make complete pattern.

L

Match on line to make complete pattern.

L

J

Match on line to make complete pattern.

West Quoddy Head Light Appliqué Pattern

Owl's Head Light

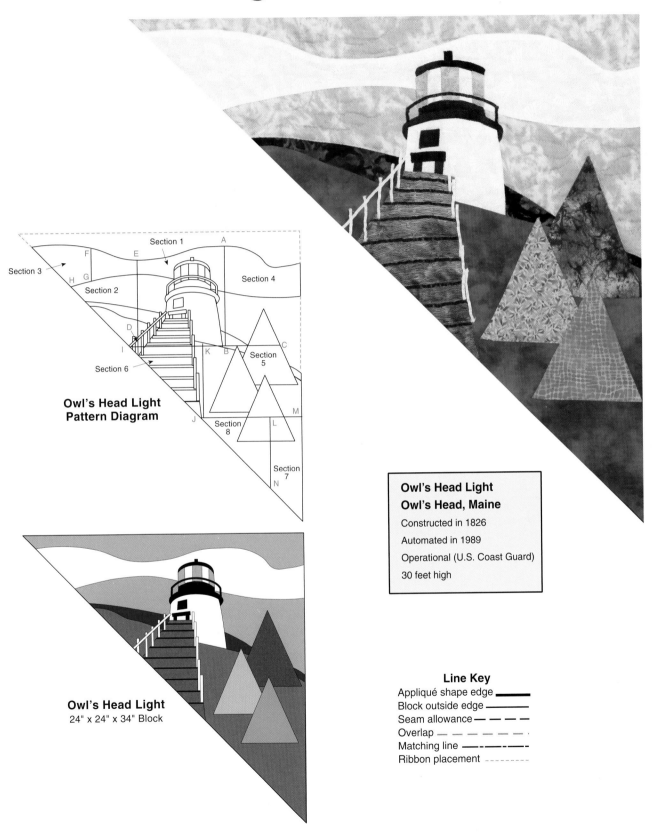

Owl's Head Light
Pattern Diagram

Section 1
Section 2
Section 3
Section 4
Section 5
Section 6
Section 7
Section 8

A
B
C
D
E
F
G
H
I
J
K
L
M
N

Owl's Head Light
24" x 24" x 34" Block

Owl's Head Light
Owl's Head, Maine

Constructed in 1826

Automated in 1989

Operational (U.S. Coast Guard)

30 feet high

Line Key
Appliqué shape edge ————
Block outside edge ————
Seam allowance — — — —
Overlap — — — — —
Matching line —·—·—·—
Ribbon placement ·········

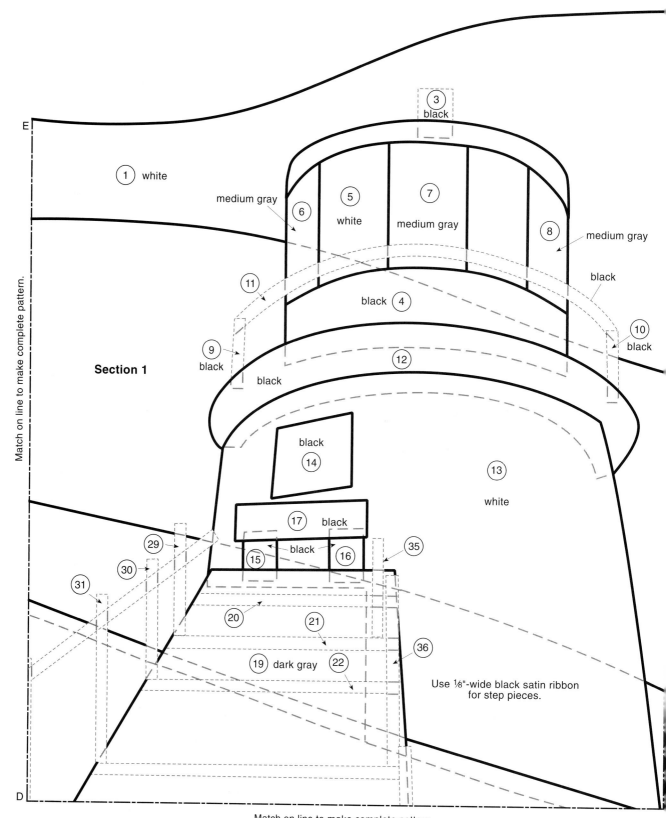

E

① white

medium gray

③ black

⑥ ⑤ white ⑦ medium gray

⑧ medium gray

black

⑪ black ④ ⑫ ⑩ black

Section 1 ⑨ black black

black ⑭ ⑬ white

⑰ black

㉙ ⑮ black ⑯ ㉟

㉚ ㊱

㉛ ⑳ ㉑

Use ⅛"-wide black satin ribbon for step pieces.

⑲ dark gray ㉒

D

Match on line to make complete pattern.
Match on line to make complete pattern.

Owl's Head Light Appliqué Pattern

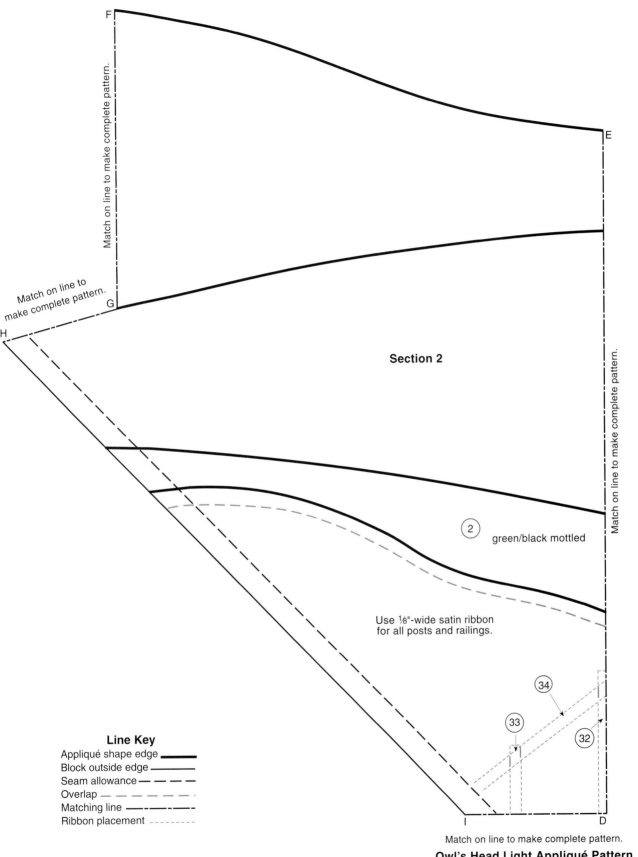

F

Match on line to make complete pattern.

E

Match on line to
make complete pattern.

G

H

Section 2

Match on line to make complete pattern.

(2) green/black mottled

Use ⅛"-wide satin ribbon
for all posts and railings.

(34)

(33)

(32)

Line Key

Appliqué shape edge	▬▬▬
Block outside edge	————
Seam allowance	— — —
Overlap	– – – –
Matching line	—·—·—
Ribbon placement	- - - -

I

D

Match on line to make complete pattern.

Owl's Head Light Appliqué Pattern

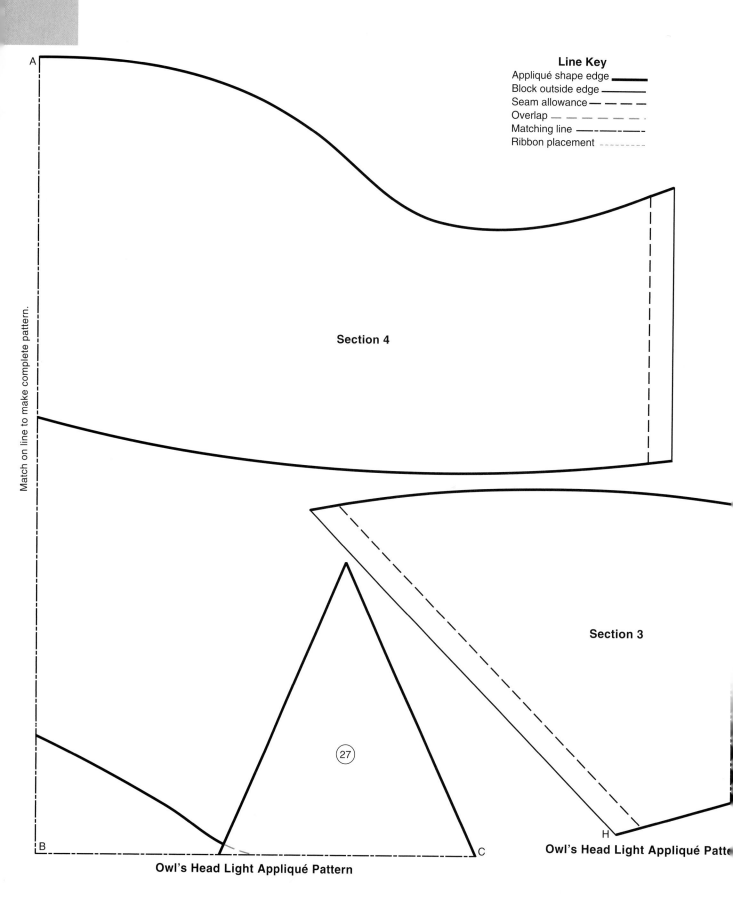

Line Key
Appliqué shape edge
Block outside edge
Seam allowance
Overlap
Matching line
Ribbon placement

Match on line to make complete pattern.

A

Section 4

Section 3

27

B

C

H

Owl's Head Light Appliqué Pattern

Owl's Head Light Appliqué Patte

HOUSE OF WHITE BIRCHES, BERNE, INDIANA 46711   WWW.WHITEBIRCHES.COM

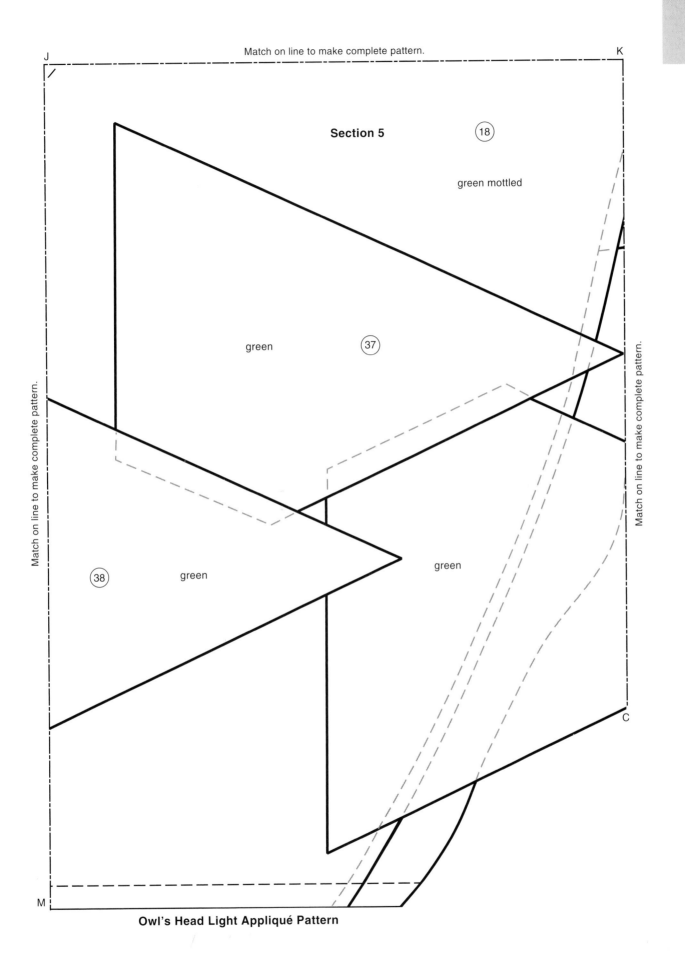

J   K

Section 5   ⑱

green mottled

green   �37

㊳ green

green

C

M

Owl's Head Light Appliqué Pattern

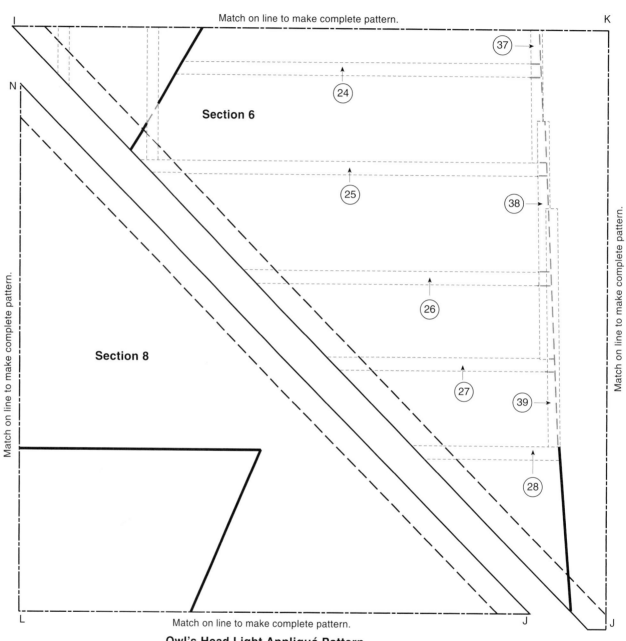

Match on line to make complete pattern.

I   K

37

N

24

Section 6

25

38

Match on line to make complete pattern.

Match on line to make complete pattern.

26

Section 8

27

39

28

L   J   J

Match on line to make complete pattern.

Owl's Head Light Appliqué Pattern

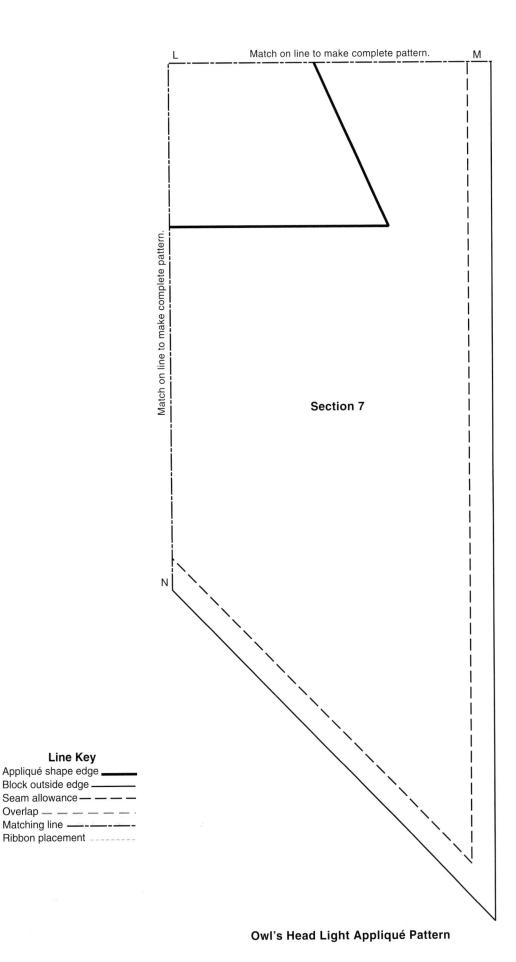

Match on line to make complete pattern.

L   M

Match on line to make complete pattern.

Section 7

N

Line Key
Appliqué shape edge ▬▬▬▬
Block outside edge ───────
Seam allowance ─ ─ ─ ─
Overlap ─ ── ─ ── ─ ·
Matching line ─·─·─·─·
Ribbon placement ··········

Owl's Head Light Appliqué Pattern

Bear Island Light

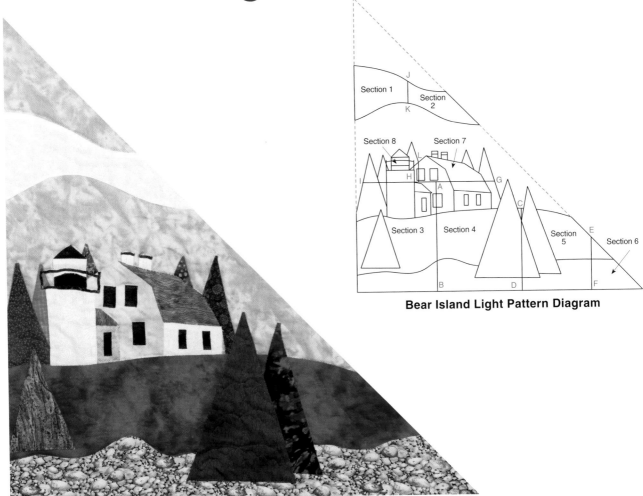

Bear Island Light Pattern Diagram

Section 1
Section 2
Section 8
Section 7
Section 3
Section 4
Section 5
Section 6

Bear Island Light
Near Northeast Harbor, Maine
Constructed in 1889
Operational (Friends of Acadia)
31 feet high

Line Key
Appliqué shape edge
Block outside edge
Seam allowance
Overlap
Matching line
Ribbon placement

Bear Island Light
24" x 24" x 34" Block

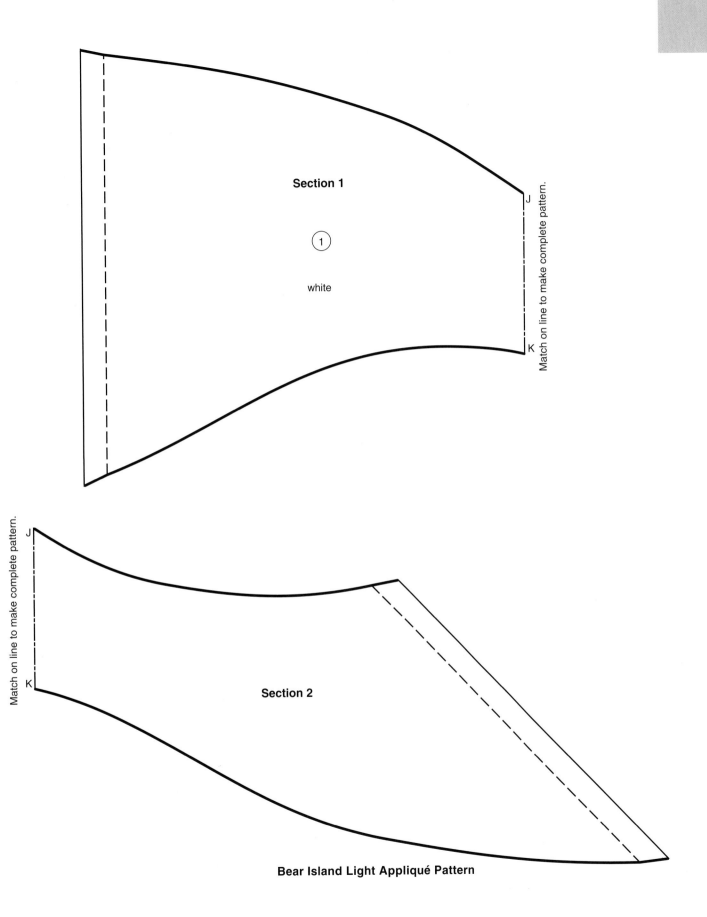

Section 1

1

white

Match on line to make complete pattern.

J

K

Match on line to make complete pattern.

J

K

Section 2

Bear Island Light Appliqué Pattern

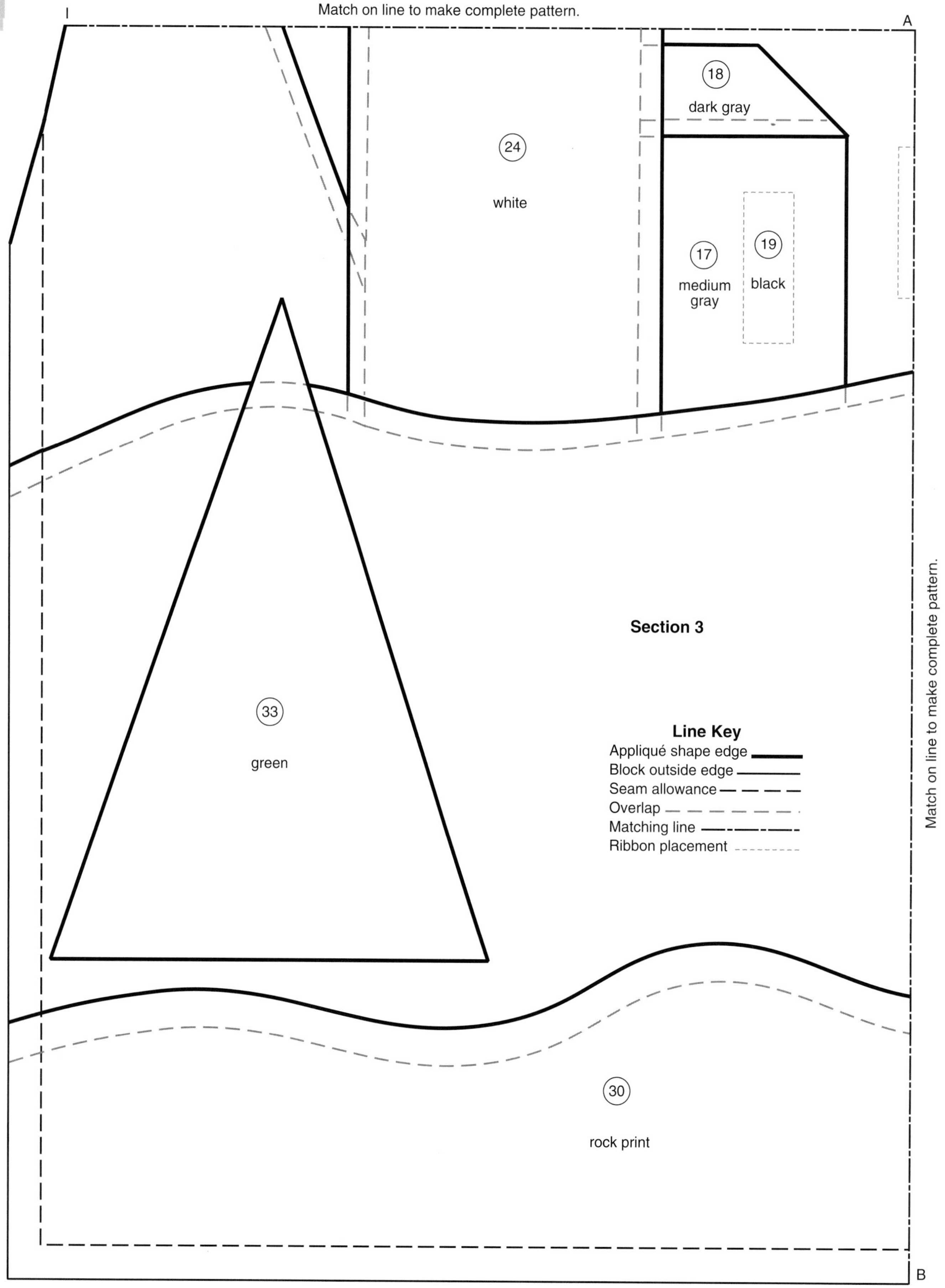

I

A

18
dark gray

24
white

17
medium gray

19
black

Section 3

33
green

Line Key

Appliqué shape edge ———
Block outside edge ———
Seam allowance — — —
Overlap — — —
Matching line —·—·—
Ribbon placement ----

30
rock print

B

Bear Island Light Appliqué Pattern

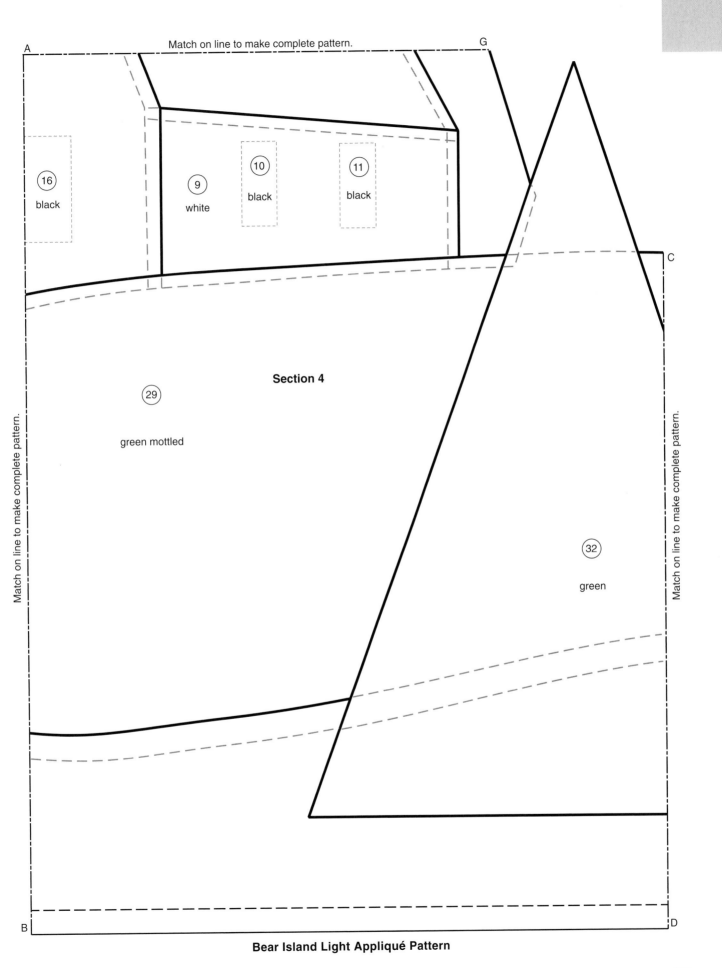

Match on line to make complete pattern.

A   G

16 black

9 white

10 black

11 black

Match on line to make complete pattern.

Match on line to make complete pattern.

Section 4

29

green mottled

C

32

green

B   D

Bear Island Light Appliqué Pattern

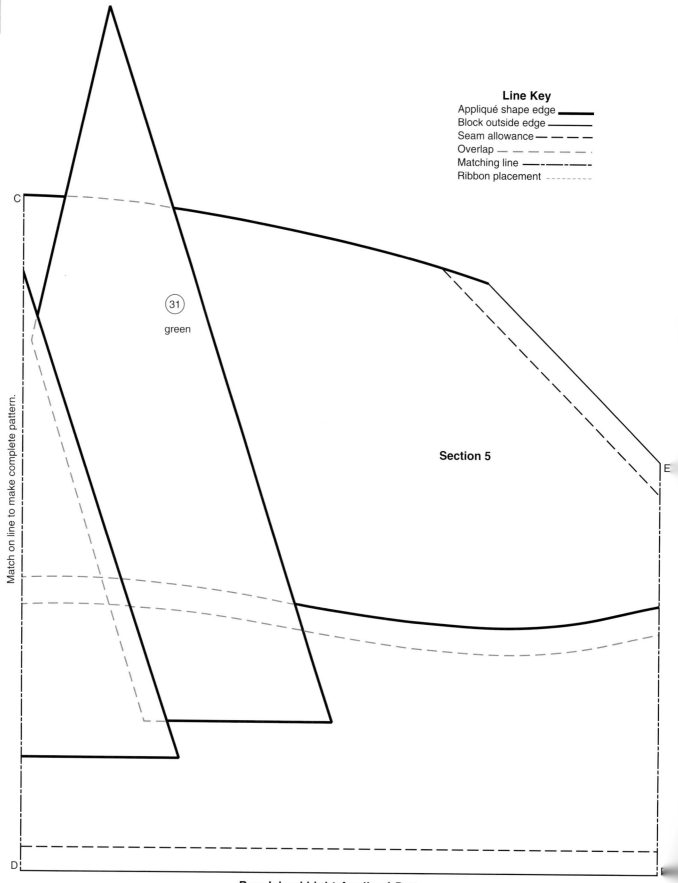

Line Key
Appliqué shape edge ▬▬▬
Block outside edge ————
Seam allowance — — —
Overlap ‑ ‑ ‑ ‑
Matching line —·—·—·
Ribbon placement ‑‑‑‑‑‑‑

C

(31)
green

Match on line to make complete pattern.

Section 5

E

D

Bear Island Light Appliqué Pattern

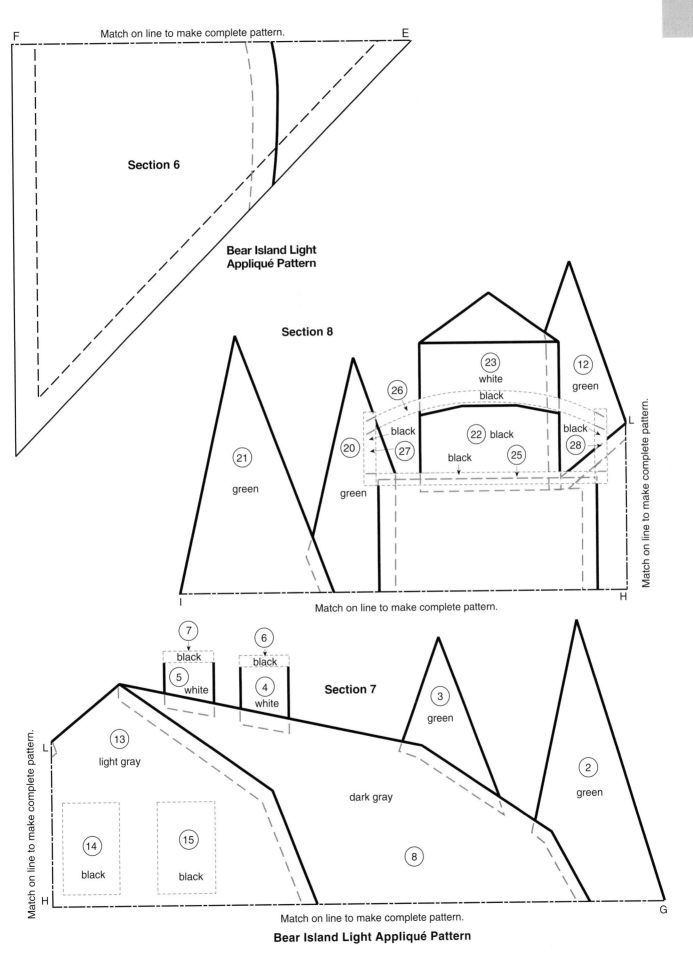

F — Match on line to make complete pattern. — E

Section 6

**Bear Island Light
Appliqué Pattern**

Section 8

㉓ white
black
⑫ green
㉖
black
⑳ green
black ㉗
㉒ black
㉕
black
㉘ black
L
Match on line to make complete pattern.
㉑ green

I — Match on line to make complete pattern. — H

⑦
black
⑤ white
⑥
black
④ white

Section 7

③ green
② green

L
⑬ light gray
dark gray

Match on line to make complete pattern.

⑭ black
⑮ black

⑧

H — Match on line to make complete pattern. — G

Bear Island Light Appliqué Pattern

Bass Harbor Head Light

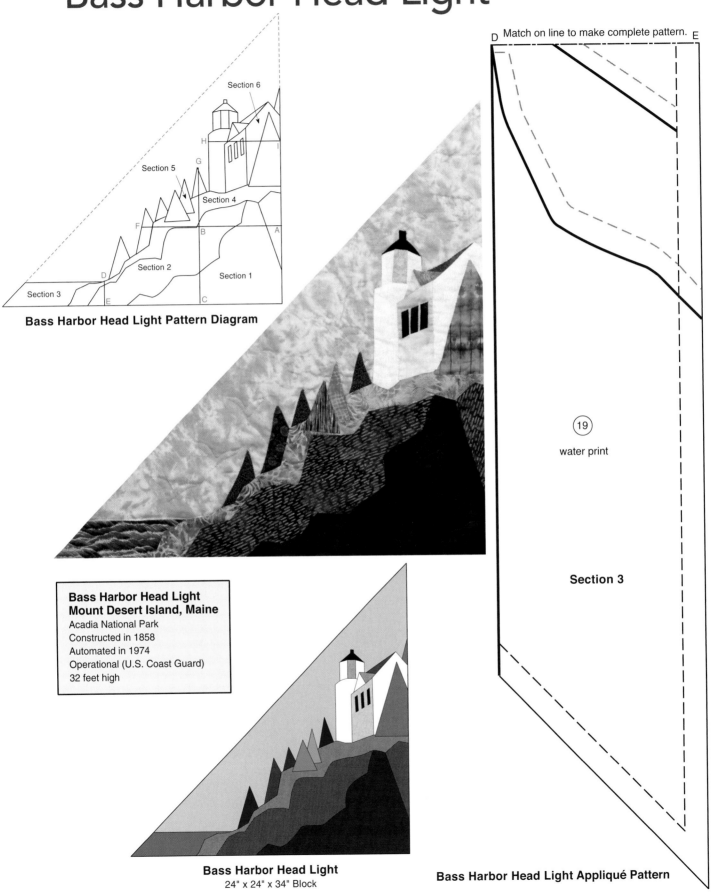

Match on line to make complete pattern.

D   E

(19)
water print

Section 3

Section 6
Section 5
Section 4
H   I
G
F   B   A
Section 2
D
Section 3   E   C
Section 1

Bass Harbor Head Light Pattern Diagram

**Bass Harbor Head Light
Mount Desert Island, Maine**
Acadia National Park
Constructed in 1858
Automated in 1974
Operational (U.S. Coast Guard)
32 feet high

Bass Harbor Head Light
24" x 24" x 34" Block

Bass Harbor Head Light Appliqué Pattern

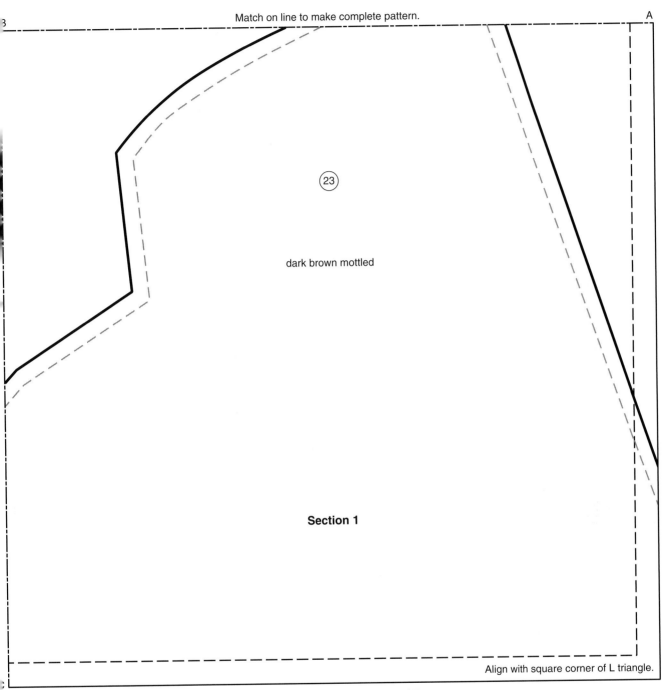

Match on line to make complete pattern.

B

A

(23)

dark brown mottled

Section 1

Align with square corner of L triangle.

Bass Harbor Head Light Appliqué Pattern

Line Key
Appliqué shape edge ▬▬▬
Block outside edge ─────
Seam allowance ─ ─ ─ ─
Overlap ─ ─ ─ ─ ─ ·
Matching line ─ · ─ · ─ · ─ ·
Ribbon placement - - - - - - -

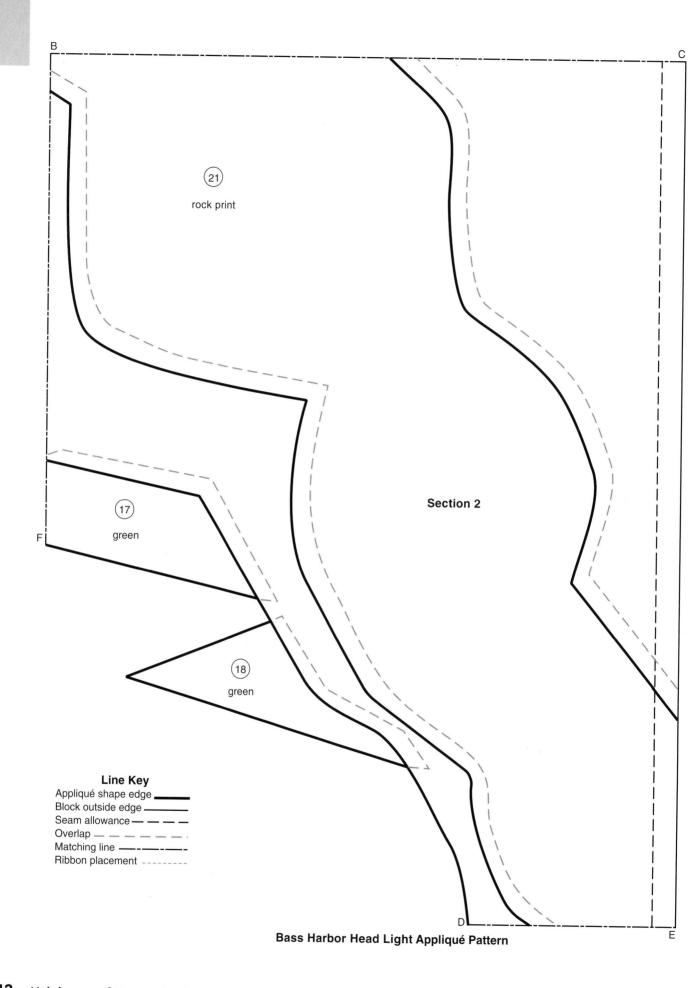

B

C

(21)
rock print

(17)
green

F

Section 2

(18)
green

Line Key
Appliqué shape edge ▬▬▬
Block outside edge ▬▬▬
Seam allowance ▬ ▬ ▬
Overlap ▬ ▬ ▬
Matching line ▬ · ▬ · ▬
Ribbon placement ┄┄┄┄

D

E

Bass Harbor Head Light Appliqué Pattern

HOUSE OF WHITE BIRCHES, BERNE, INDIANA 46711   WWW.WHITEBIRCHES.COM

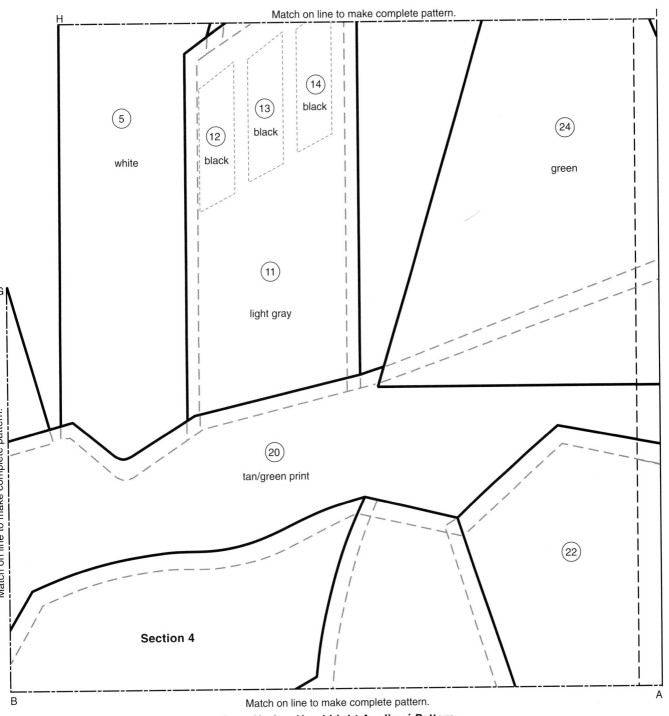

Match on line to make complete pattern.

H

⑤ white

⑫ black

⑬ black

⑭ black

⑪ light gray

㉔ green

⑳ tan/green print

㉒

Section 4

B

Match on line to make complete pattern.

Bass Harbor Head Light Appliqué Pattern

I

A

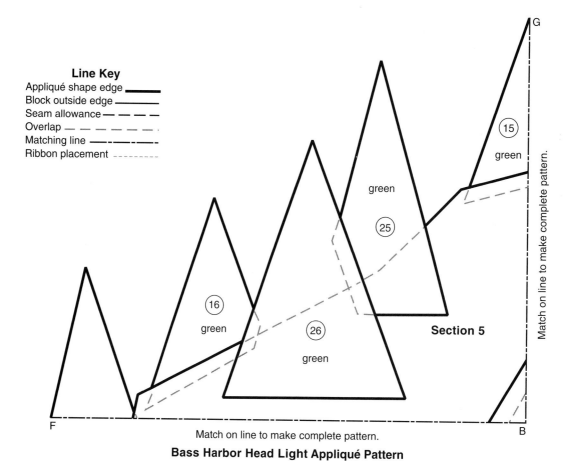

Line Key
Appliqué shape edge ▬▬▬
Block outside edge ▬▬▬
Seam allowance ▬ ▬ ▬
Overlap ▬ ▬ ▬
Matching line ▬·▬·▬
Ribbon placement ·······

15 green

25 green

16 green

26 green

Section 5

Match on line to make complete pattern.

G

F

B

Match on line to make complete pattern.

Bass Harbor Head Light Appliqué Pattern

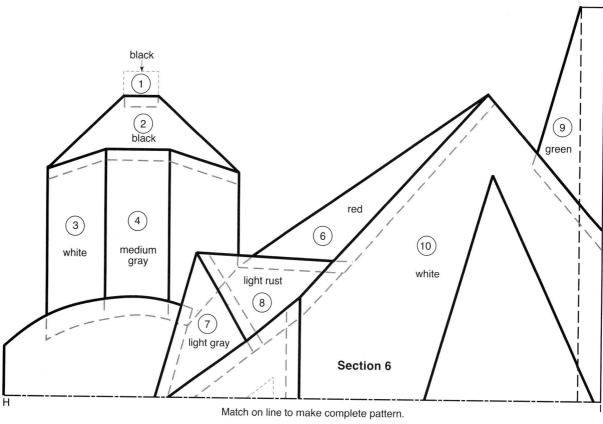

black

1

2 black

3 white

4 medium gray

red

6

9 green

10 white

light rust

8

7 light gray

Section 6

H

Match on line to make complete pattern.

Pemaquid Point Light

Pemaquid Point Light
Pemaquid Point, Maine

Constructed in 1835

Operational (U.S. Coast Guard)

38 feet high

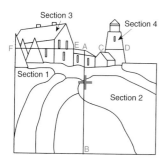

Pemaquid Point Light
Pattern Diagram

Line Key

Appliqué shape edge ——————
Block outside edge ——————
Seam allowance — — — —
Overlap — — — — — ·
Matching line ——·——·——
Ribbon placement - - - - - - -
Center mark +

Pemaquid Point Light
12" x 12" Block

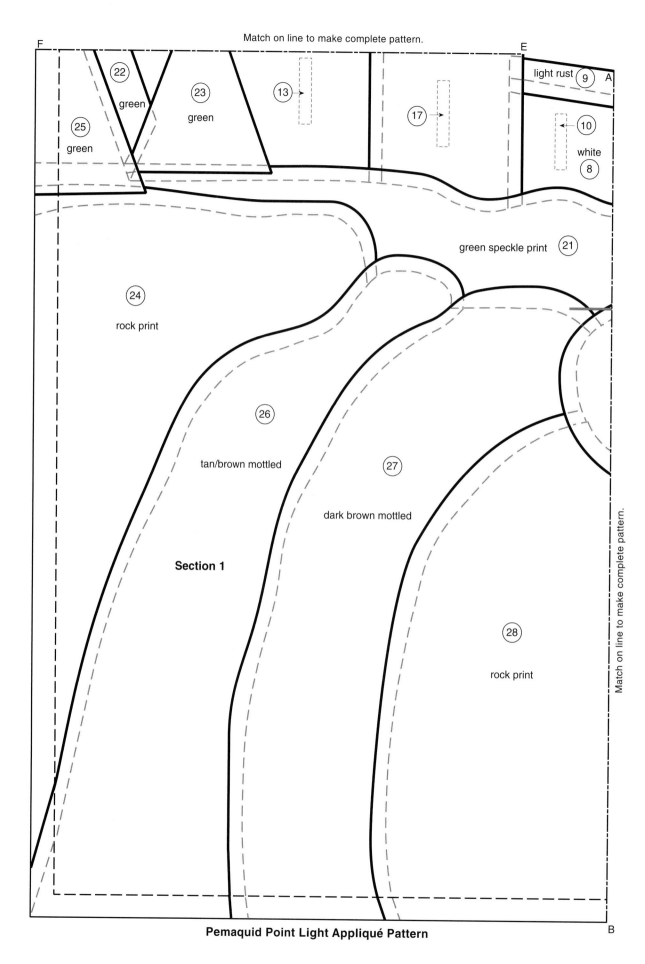

Match on line to make complete pattern.

F
E
A

22 green

23 green

25 green

13

17

light rust 9

10

white 8

green speckle print 21

24 rock print

26 tan/brown mottled

27 dark brown mottled

Section 1

28 rock print

Match on line to make complete pattern.

B

Pemaquid Point Light Appliqué Pattern

HOUSE OF WHITE BIRCHES, BERNE, INDIANA 46711   WWW.WHITEBIRCHES.COM

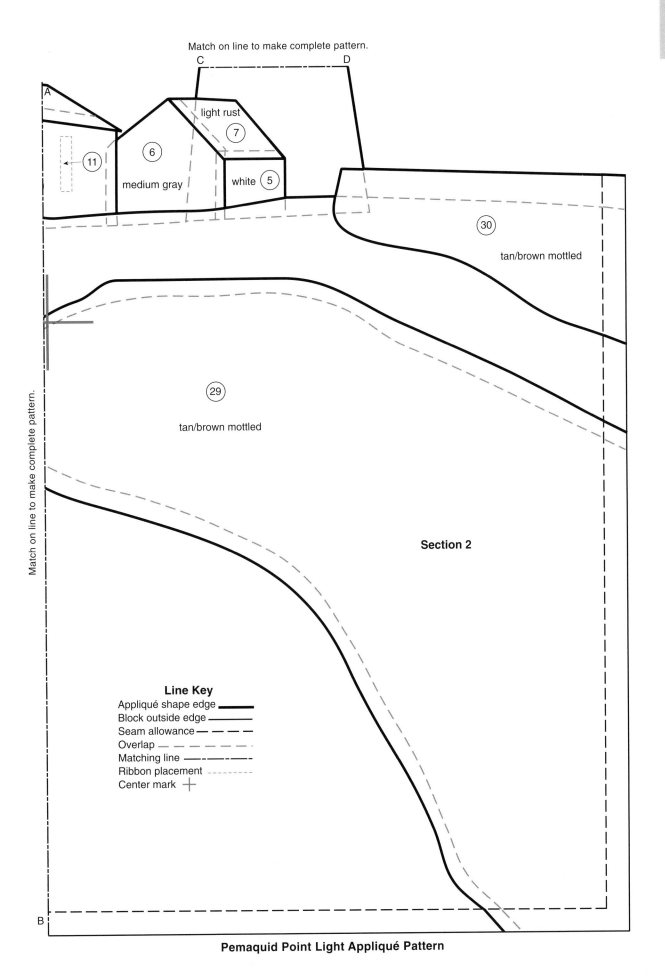

Match on line to make complete pattern.

C   D

A

light rust

⑦

⑥   ⑪

medium gray   white ⑤

㉚

tan/brown mottled

Match on line to make complete pattern.

㉙

tan/brown mottled

Section 2

Line Key
Appliqué shape edge ——————
Block outside edge ——————
Seam allowance — — — — —
Overlap — — — — — —
Matching line —·—·—·—·—
Ribbon placement ···········
Center mark ✛

B

Pemaquid Point Light Appliqué Pattern

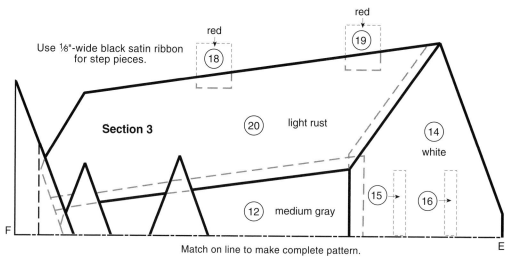

Use ⅛"-wide black satin ribbon for step pieces.

red
(18)

red
(19)

Section 3

(20) light rust

F

(14)
white

(15) → (16) →

(12) medium gray

Match on line to make complete pattern.

Pemaquid Point Light Appliqué Pattern

E

Line Key
Appliqué shape edge ——————
Block outside edge ——————
Seam allowance — — — —
Overlap — — — — — ·
Matching line ——·——·——
Ribbon placement ----------

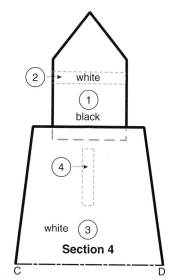

(2) → white

(1)
black

(4) →

white (3)

Section 4

C D

Match on line to make complete pattern.

Dice Head

Dice Head Light
Castine, Maine

Constructed in 1829

Automated in 1989

No longer operational (private residence)

27 feet high

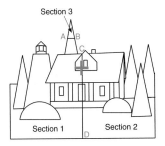

Dice Head Light
Pattern Diagram

Line Key

Appliqué shape edge ▬▬▬▬

Block outside edge _____

Seam allowance — — — —

Overlap ― ― — — —

Matching line —·—·—·—

Ribbon placement ············

Center mark ┼

Dice Head Light
12" x 12" Block

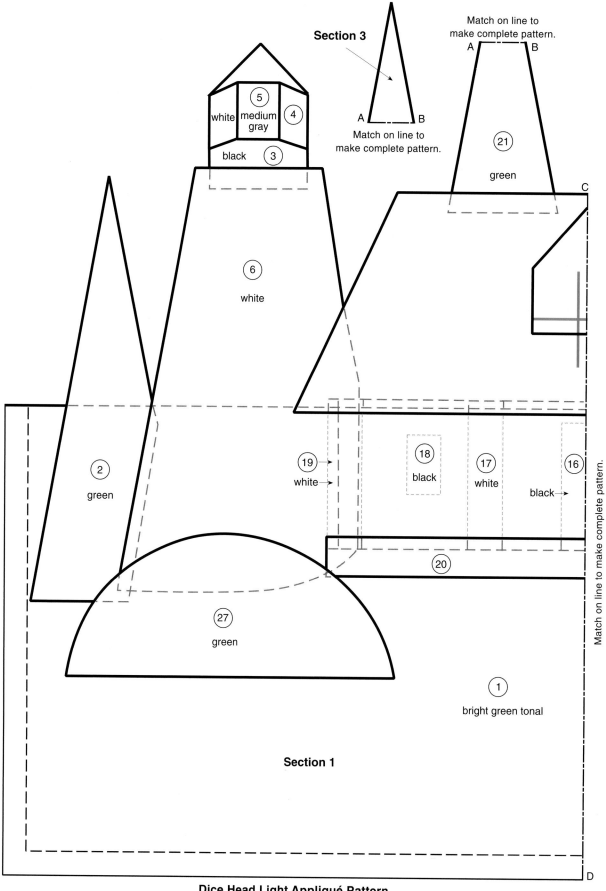

Section 3

Match on line to make complete pattern.

A   B

Match on line to make complete pattern.

⑤ white · medium gray · ④

black · ③

② green

⑥ white

㉑ green

⑲ white

⑱ black

⑰ white

⑯ black →

⑳

㉗ green

① bright green tonal

Section 1

Match on line to make complete pattern.

Dice Head Light Appliqué Pattern

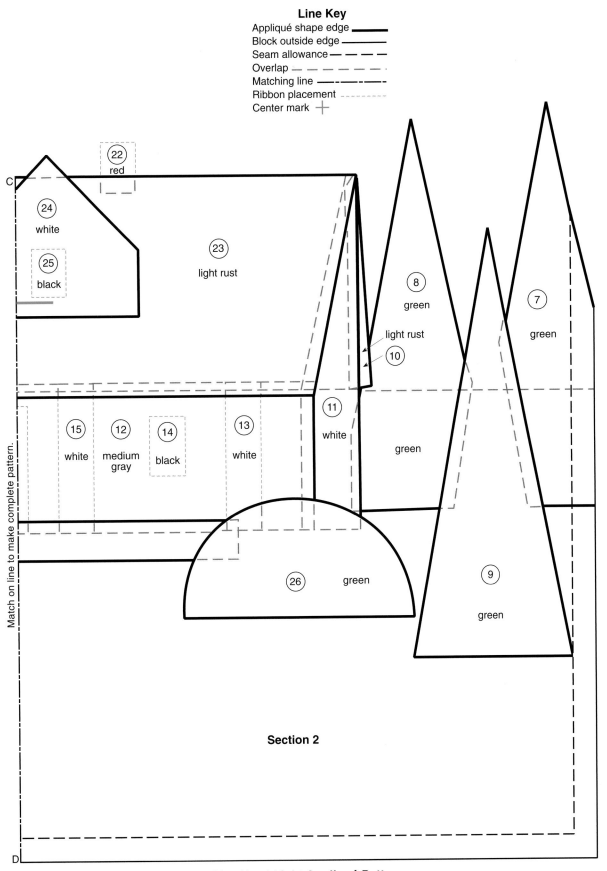

Line Key

Appliqué shape edge ———
Block outside edge ———
Seam allowance — — —
Overlap ⸺ ⸺ ⸺
Matching line —·—·—·
Ribbon placement ········
Center mark +

(22) red

C

(24) white

(25) black

(23) light rust

(8) green

(7) green

light rust

(10)

(11) white

green

Match on line to make complete pattern.

(15) white

(12) medium gray

(14) black

(13) white

(26) green

(9) green

Section 2

D

Dice Head Light Appliqué Pattern

Portland Head Light

Portland Head Light
Cape Elizabeth, Maine

Constructed in 1791 by order of George Washington

Automated in 1989

Operational (Town of Cape Elizabeth)

80 feet high

Line Key

Appliqué shape edge ━━━━

Block outside edge ━━━━━

Seam allowance ━ ━ ━ ━

Overlap ━ ━ ━ ━ ━ ·

Matching line ━━ ·━ ·━ ·

Ribbon placement - - - - - -

Center mark ┼

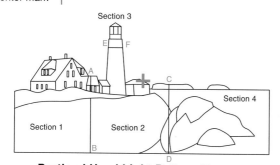

Portland Head Light Pattern Diagram

Portland Head Light
12" x 22" Block

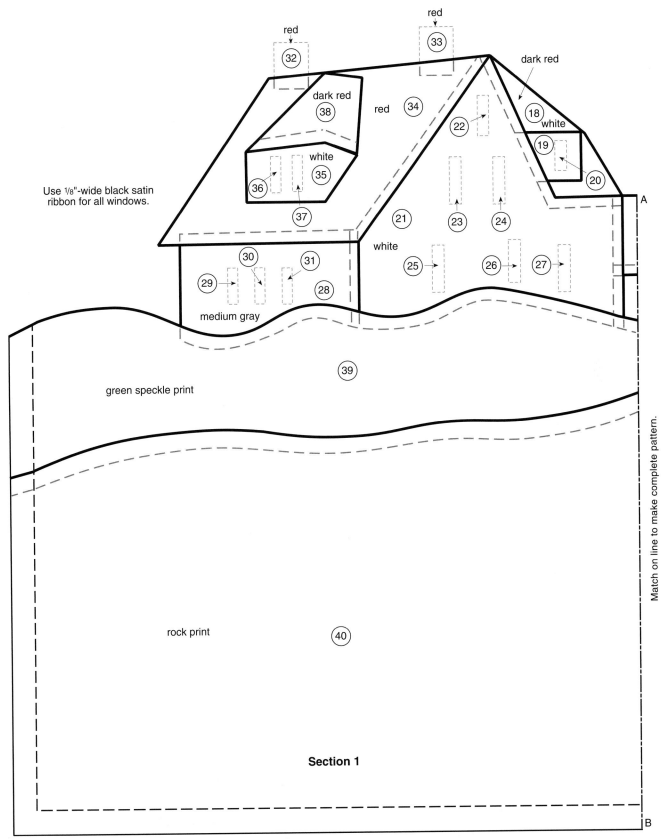

Use 1/8"-wide black satin ribbon for all windows.

Section 1

Portland Head Light Appliqué Pattern

red · red · dark red · dark red · white · red · white · white · medium gray · green speckle print · rock print

Match on line to make complete pattern.

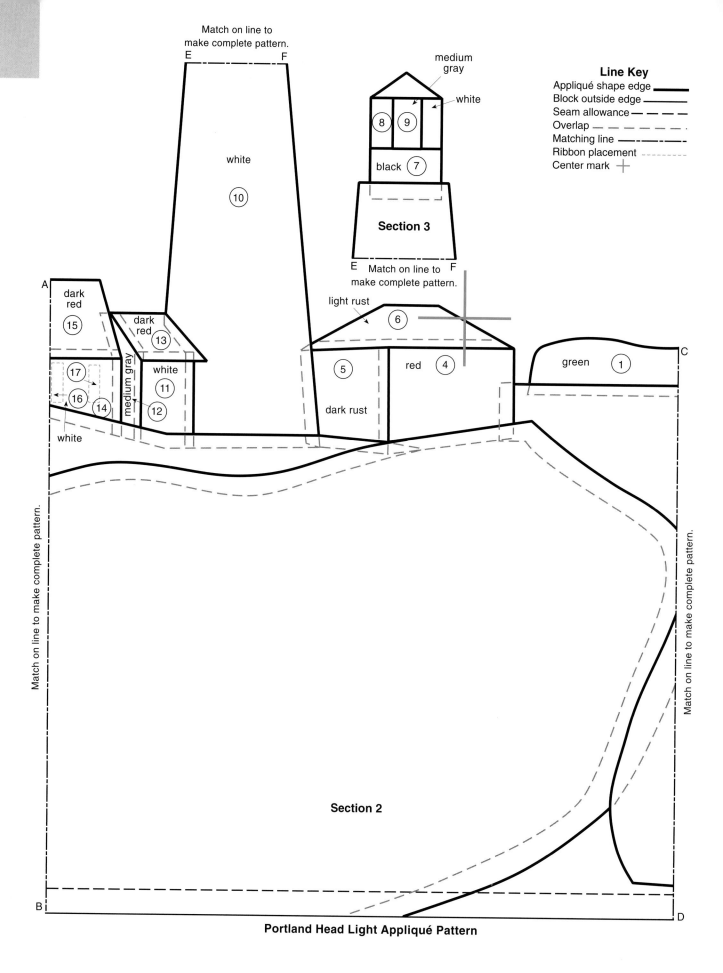

Match on line to make complete pattern.

E   F

white

(10)

medium gray

white

(8) (9)

black (7)

Section 3

E Match on line to make complete pattern. F

Line Key
Appliqué shape edge
Block outside edge
Seam allowance
Overlap
Matching line
Ribbon placement
Center mark +

A

dark red (15)

dark red (13)

medium gray

white (11)

(12)

white

(17)

(16) (14)

light rust

(6)

(5)

dark rust

red (4)

green (1)

C

Match on line to make complete pattern.

Match on line to make complete pattern.

Section 2

B   D

Portland Head Light Appliqué Pattern

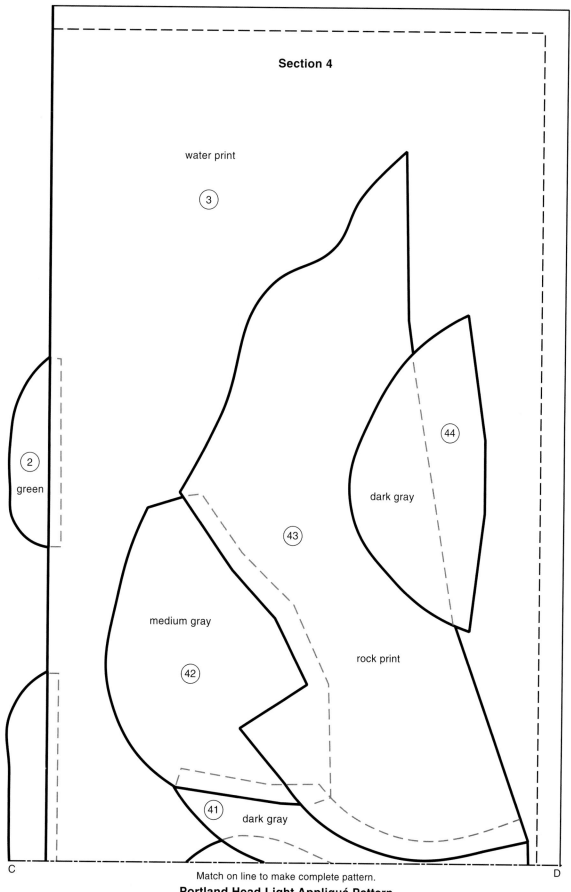

Section 4

water print

③

②

green

④④

dark gray

④③

medium gray

④②

rock print

④① dark gray

C

D

Match on line to make complete pattern.

Portland Head Light Appliqué Pattern

Fort Point Light

Fort Point Light
Stockton Springs, Maine

Constructed in 1857

Operational (State of Maine)

31 feet high

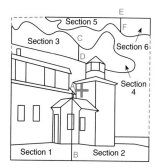

Fort Point Light
Pattern Diagram

Line Key
Appliqué shape edge
Block outside edge
Seam allowance
Overlap
Matching line
Ribbon placement
Center mark

Fort Point Light
12" x 12" Block

HOUSE OF WHITE BIRCHES, BERNE, INDIANA 46711   WWW.WHITEBIRCHES.COM

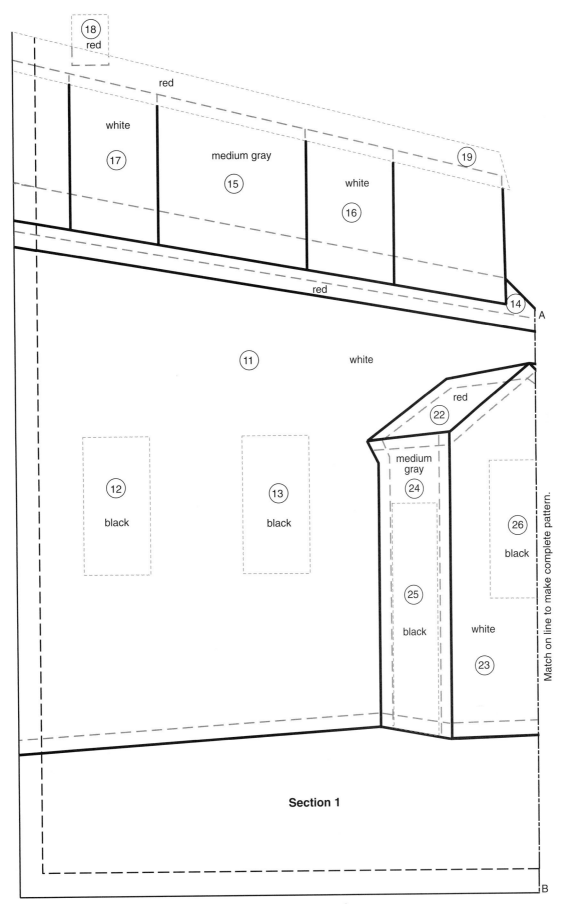

Fort Point Light Appliqué Pattern

18 red

red

white

17

medium gray

15

white

16

19

red

14

A

11

white

22

red

12

black

13

black

medium gray

24

26

black

25

black

23

white

Match on line to make complete pattern.

Section 1

B

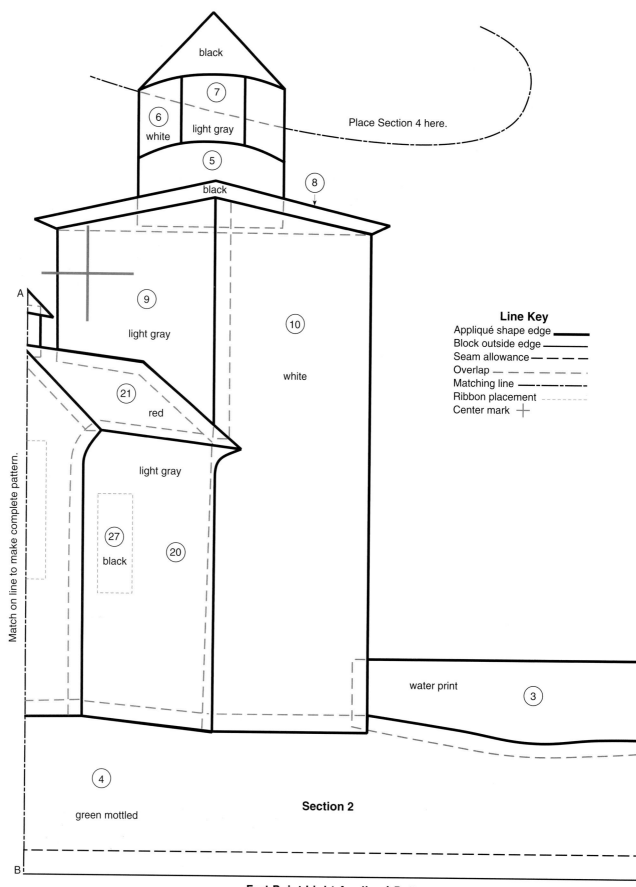

black

7

6

white

light gray

5

black

8

Place Section 4 here.

Line Key
Appliqué shape edge
Block outside edge
Seam allowance
Overlap
Matching line
Ribbon placement
Center mark

A

9

light gray

10

white

21

red

light gray

Match on line to make complete pattern.

27

black

20

water print

3

4

green mottled

Section 2

B

Fort Point Light Appliqué Pattern

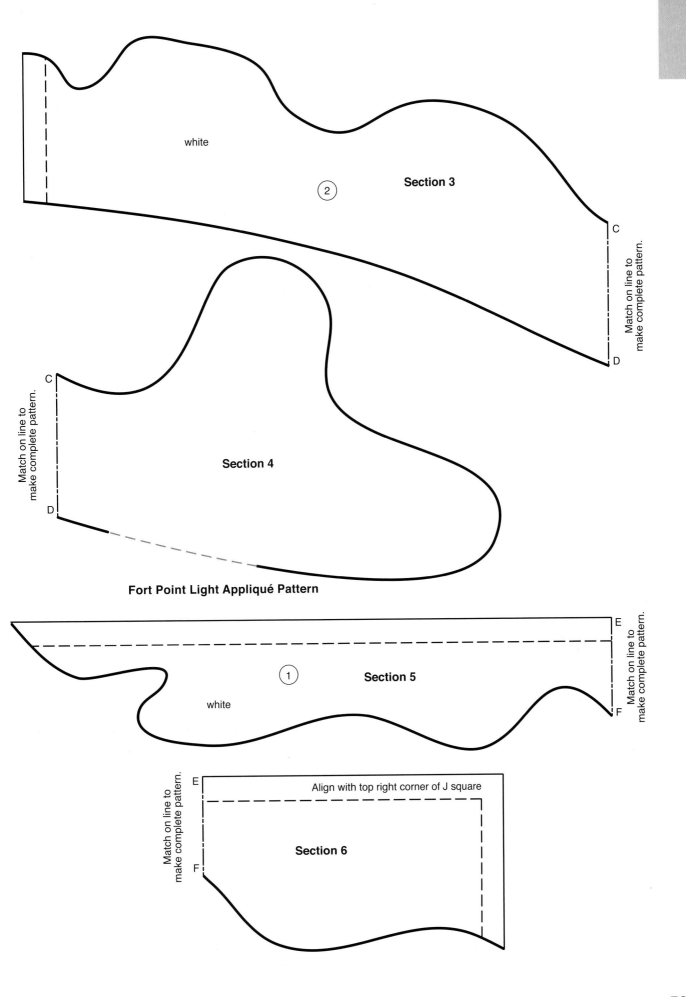

white

②   **Section 3**

C

D

Match on line to make complete pattern.

C

Match on line to make complete pattern.

D

Section 4

Fort Point Light Appliqué Pattern

E

①   **Section 5**

white

F

Match on line to make complete pattern.

E

Align with top right corner of J square

Match on line to make complete pattern.

F

Section 6

Eagle Island Wall Quilt

Maine's Eagle Island Light stands on the northeast tip of Eagle Island in East Penobscot Bay. The light was activated in 1858. In 1959, the tower was automated and is still an active aid to navigation.

The U.S. Coast Guard took over the station in 1945, and the keeper's house was demolished. The 1,200-pound fog bell toppled over the cliff into the ocean, was salvaged by a local caretaker and dragged by lobster boat to Spruce Head, where it still can be found.

This wall quilt shows how dramatically fabric choices can affect the look of your quilt. The four blocks are identical except for the colors used. You can use scraps from your stash to create seasonal scenes as I did, or try a different theme such as varying weather conditions or times of day.

Eagle Island Light
9" x 12" Block

PROJECT SPECIFICATIONS
Skill Level: Intermediate
Quilt Size: 27" x 33"
Block Size: 9" x 12"
Number of Blocks: 4

FABRIC & BATTING
- Scraps for appliqué and piecing
- 4 (9½" x 12½") F rectangles sky fabrics
- 1 fat quarter water print
- ⅓ yard blue/green metallic batik
- ½ yard dark blue mottled
- Backing 33" x 39"
- Batting 33" x 39"

SUPPLIES & TOOLS
- All-purpose thread to match fabrics
- Quilting thread
- 1 yard fusible web
- Water-erasable marker or chalk pencil
- Basic sewing tools and supplies

INSTRUCTIONS
Cutting
Step 1. Cut a variety of 1½"-wide A strips from scraps used in the appliqué. **Note:** *You may need to make more strip sets or cut a few 1½" squares to have enough segments, depending on the sizes of your remaining pieces.*

Step 2. Cut (12) 1½" x 9½" B strips and (12) 1½" x 12½" C strips dark blue mottled.

Step 3. Cut nine 3½" x 3½" D squares water print.

Step 4. Cut a 7" x 11" rectangle fusible web; fuse to the wrong side of the water print. Cut four

1½" x 9½" E strips from fused section; remove paper backing.

Step 5. Select fabrics for appliqué blocks. *Note: Have fun looking through your scrap stash for prints and colors that will add interest to your quilt. One of the fabrics I used is actually a birdseed print, but it looks like rocks from a distance! You may find a blue batik that's perfect for a stormy sky or some grays for a foggy scene.*

Step 6. Cut and prepare appliqué pieces referring to the General Instructions for Appliqué on page 4. *Note: The sample quilt shown was machine-appliquéd.*

Step 7. Cut four 2¼" by fabric width strips blue/green metallic batik for binding.

Appliqué Blocks

Step 1. Create four appliquéd Eagle Island Light blocks using the F rectangles for the background referring to the pattern given and the General Instructions for Appliqué on page 4.

Step 2. Fuse E to the bottom edge of each appliquéd unit to complete the blocks.

Completing the Top

Step 1. Sew A strips together in random order in sets of nine and 12 referring to Figure 1; subcut six 1½" segments from each strip set, again referring to Figure 1.

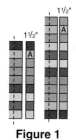

Figure 1

Make 6

Figure 2

Step 2. Sew a nine-segment strip between two B strips as shown in Figure 2; press seams toward B. Repeat for six A-B units.

Step 3. Sew a 12-segment strip between two C strips, again referring to Figure 2; press seams toward C. Repeat for six A-C units.

Step 4. Join two appliqué blocks with three A-C units to make a block row referring to Figure 3; repeat for two block rows. Press seams toward A-C units.

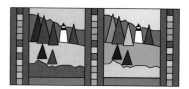

Figure 3

Step 5. Join three D squares with two A-B units to make a sashing row as shown in Figure 4; repeat for three sashing rows. Press seams toward the A-B units.

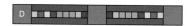

Figure 4

Eagle Island Light
Placement Diagram
27" x 33"

Step 6. Join the block rows and sashing rows referring to the Placement Diagram for positioning; press seams toward the sashing rows.

Completing the Quilt

Step 1. Sandwich batting between the completed top and prepared backing piece; pin or baste layers together to hold flat.

Step 2. Quilt as desired by hand or machine.

Step 3. When quilting is complete, remove pins or basting; trim batting and backing edges even with quilt top.

Step 4. Join binding strips on short ends to make one long strip; press seams open.

Step 5. Fold binding strip in half along length with wrong sides together; press.

Step 6. Sew binding strip to quilt top with raw edges even, mitering corners and overlapping ends. Turn binding to the back side; hand- or machine-stitch in place to finish. ■

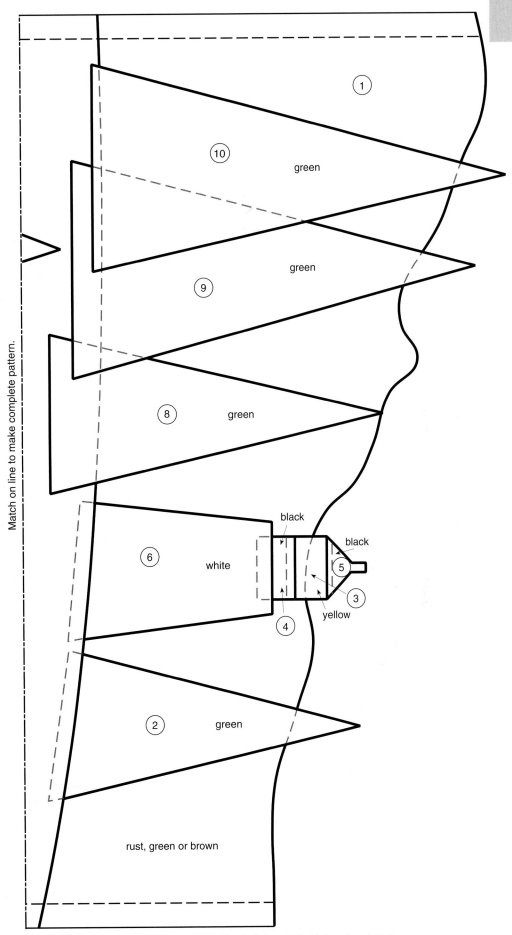

Match on line to make complete pattern.

① green
⑩ green
⑨ green
⑧ green
⑥ white
black
black
⑤
③
② green
④
yellow
rust, green or brown

Eagle Island Light Appliqué Pattern

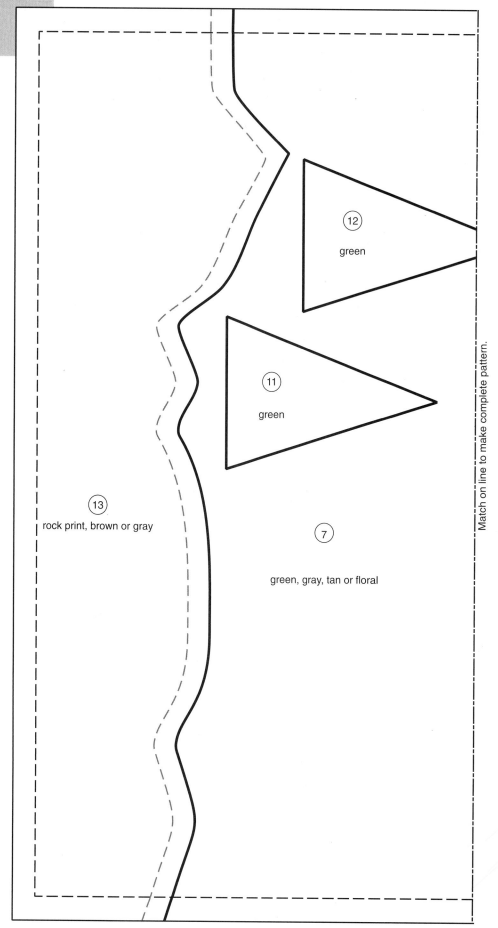

Match on line to make complete pattern.

12
green

11
green

13
rock print, brown or gray

7
green, gray, tan or floral

Eagle Island Light Appliqué Pattern

E-mail: Customer_Service@whitebirches.c[...]

Lighthouses of New England is published by House of White Birches, 306 East Parr Road, Ber[...] IN 46711, telephone (260) 589-4000. Printed in USA. Copyright © 2006 House of White Birches.

HOUSE of WHITE BIRCHES PUBLISHERS SINCE 1947

RETAIL STORES: If you would lik[...] to carry this pattern book or any[...] other House of White Birches publications, c[...] the Wholesale Department at Annie's Attic t[...] set up a direct account: (903) 636-4303. Also, request a complete listing of publications available from House of White Birches.

Every effort has been made to ensure that th[...] instructions in this pattern book are complet[...] and accurate. We cannot, however, take responsibility for human error, typographical mistakes or variations in individual work.

ISBN-10: 1-59217-108-7
ISBN-13: 978-1-59217-108-8
1 2 3 4 5 6 7 8 9

STAFF
Editors: Jeanne Stauffer, Sandra L. Hatch
Associate Editor: Dianne Schmidt
Technical Artist: Connie Rand
Copy Supervisor: Michelle Beck
Copy Editors: Sue Harvey, Nicki Lehman,
   Judy Weatherford
Graphic Arts Supervisor: Ronda Bechinski
Graphic Artists: Debby Keel, Edith Teegarden
Art Director: Brad Snow
Assistant Art Director: Nick Pierce
Photography: Tammy Christian, Don Clark,
   Matthew Owen, Jackie Schaffel
Photo Stylists: Tammy Nussbaum,
   Tammy M. Smith